Info in back

Lech Majewski

Foreword

The word "global" has left an indelible mark on our era, seeping into every niche and corner of the cultural domain through economic channels. On many a occasion, it is being discussed and accepted by designers that regional characteristics of design are fast disappearing, blurring the boundaries between works of different nations. Under this circumstance, the eyes of the public would be directly focused on the designer who possesses a distinctive, signature style. A successful designer always integrates such elements as personality, living environment, and reaction to social influence into his/her works. The designer's works also become an expression of his/her design idea, life philosophy, aesthetic value, and living experience.

The book series, "Vision of Design", is intended to help readers understand the works of these designers from the perspective of their individual circumstance and design experience. But I believe that it is the connection between life and design that lies behind this perspective. In "The Arts of Mankind", Hendrik Willem Van Loon says that "life is the noblest art of mankind." Life is indeed the ultimate source of creativity for designers!

There are five designers discussed in this first book of an oncoming series. They are Reza Abedini from Tehran, Studio Boot from Holland, Michel Bouvet from Paris, Lech Majewski from Warsaw, and István Orosz from Budapest. The story of each graphic designer shows sparkles of their wisdom.

Jianping He, Dec. 2006, Berlin

10 answers to 10 questions

1. How is design present in your life?

Design is omnipresent in my life. I design posters, books, calendars. It takes a large portion of my time.

2. Does your design inspiration come from your life experience? Where does your inspiration come from?

First of all, you must have consciousness and knowledge of how to cooperate with your ownself. Yes, it does come from my life experience, the place where I come from. It comes from the tradition of the country where I grew up. I was often influenced by others (masters) specializing in different domains of art as well as young people. Then you know how to use your experience and inspiration to find your own solution.

3. Who is the main influence in your life?

My mother is the one who recognized my skills and talent. In due time, she made decisions about suitable schools and always supported me in my attachment to fine arts.

The most significant influence on my design was Henryk Tomaszewski, my pedagogue. He tought me how to be myself in design and how to create my own visual language.

4. What is your philosophy of life? And what is your philosophy of design?

Life - Be happy and don't harm anybody.

Design - be yourself and have fun

5. Which was the happiest moment in your life?

I am trying to have lots of them in every part of my life.

6. What is your motivation to stick to the design job?

The possibility of realizing my own ideas.

7. What are your top personal achievements?

I am a modest, plain guy and I have my own porsche 911.

8. How do you manage your free time?

I like playing the guitar. I go to the cinema, theaters and concerts.

9. What are your hobbies?

Traveling and laziness.

10. When do you plan to retire and how do you plan after your retirement?

In this job you never retire. Being an artist lasts till the very end.

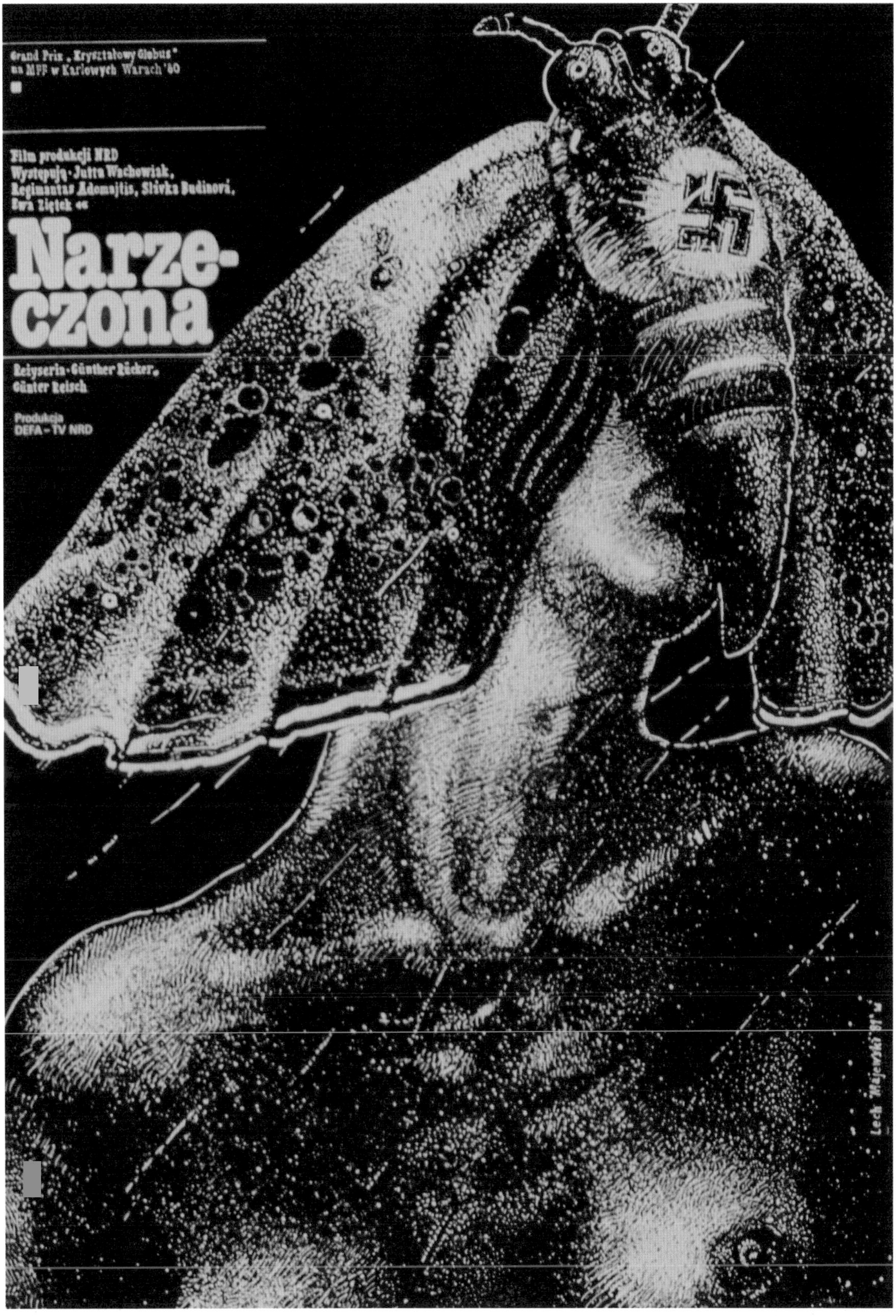

«Fiancee». Poster. 1981. 98 x 68 cm. Offset. Client: ZRF Association of Films' Distribution.

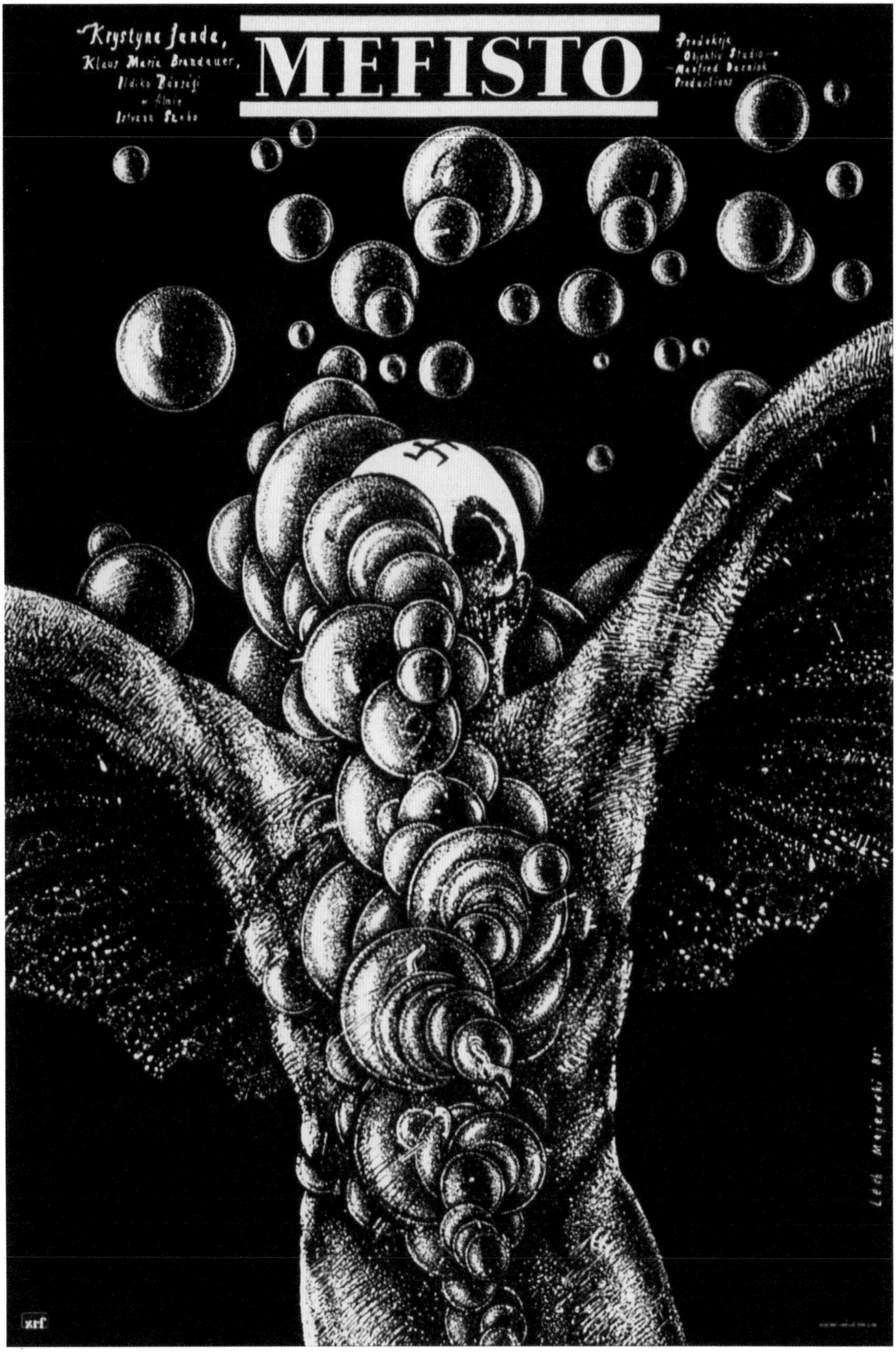

« Mefisto ». Poster. 1981. 98 x 68 cm. Offset. Client: CWF. Poster for a film.

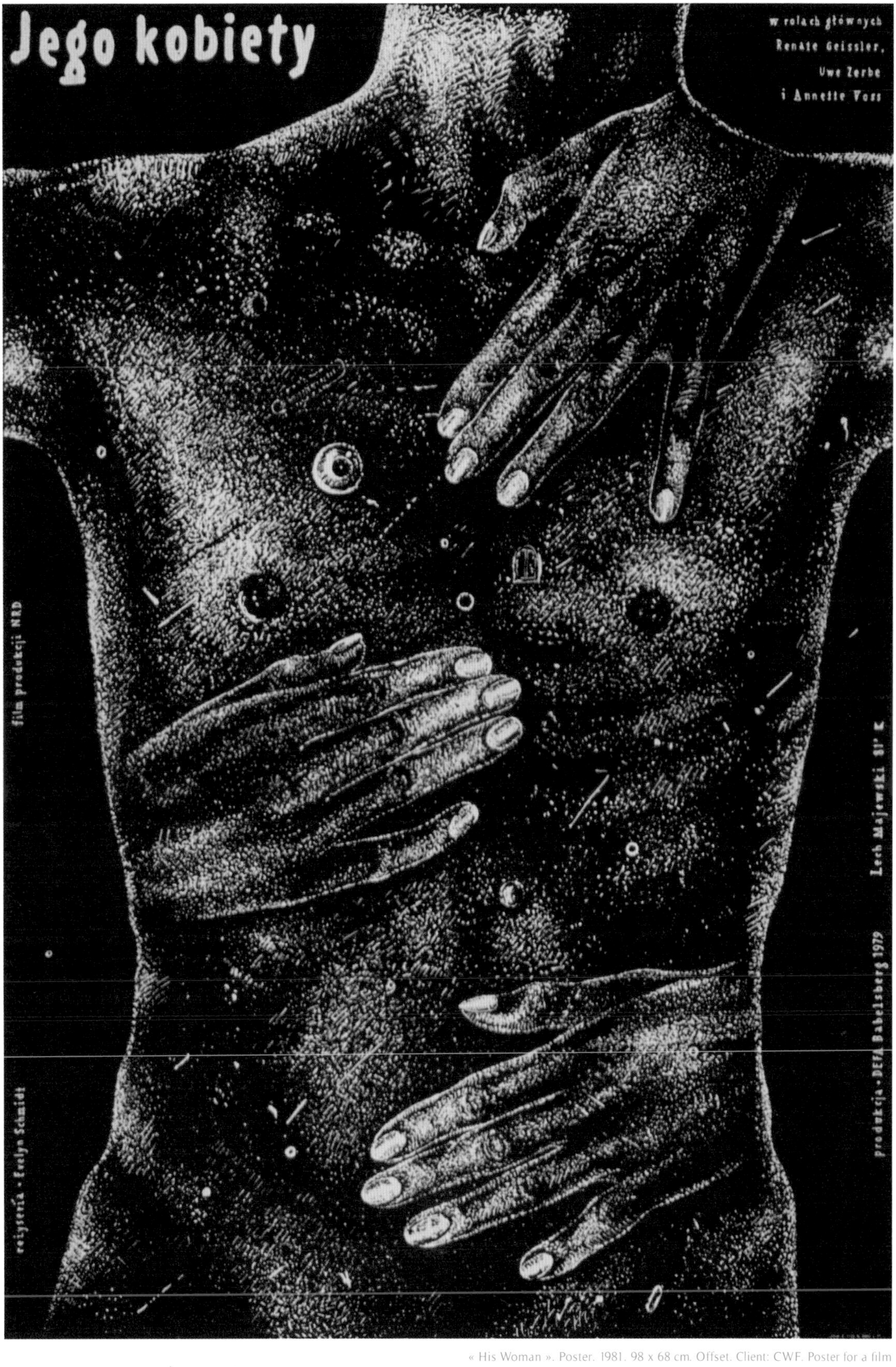

« His Woman ». Poster. 1981. 98 x 68 cm. Offset. Client: CWF. Poster for a film

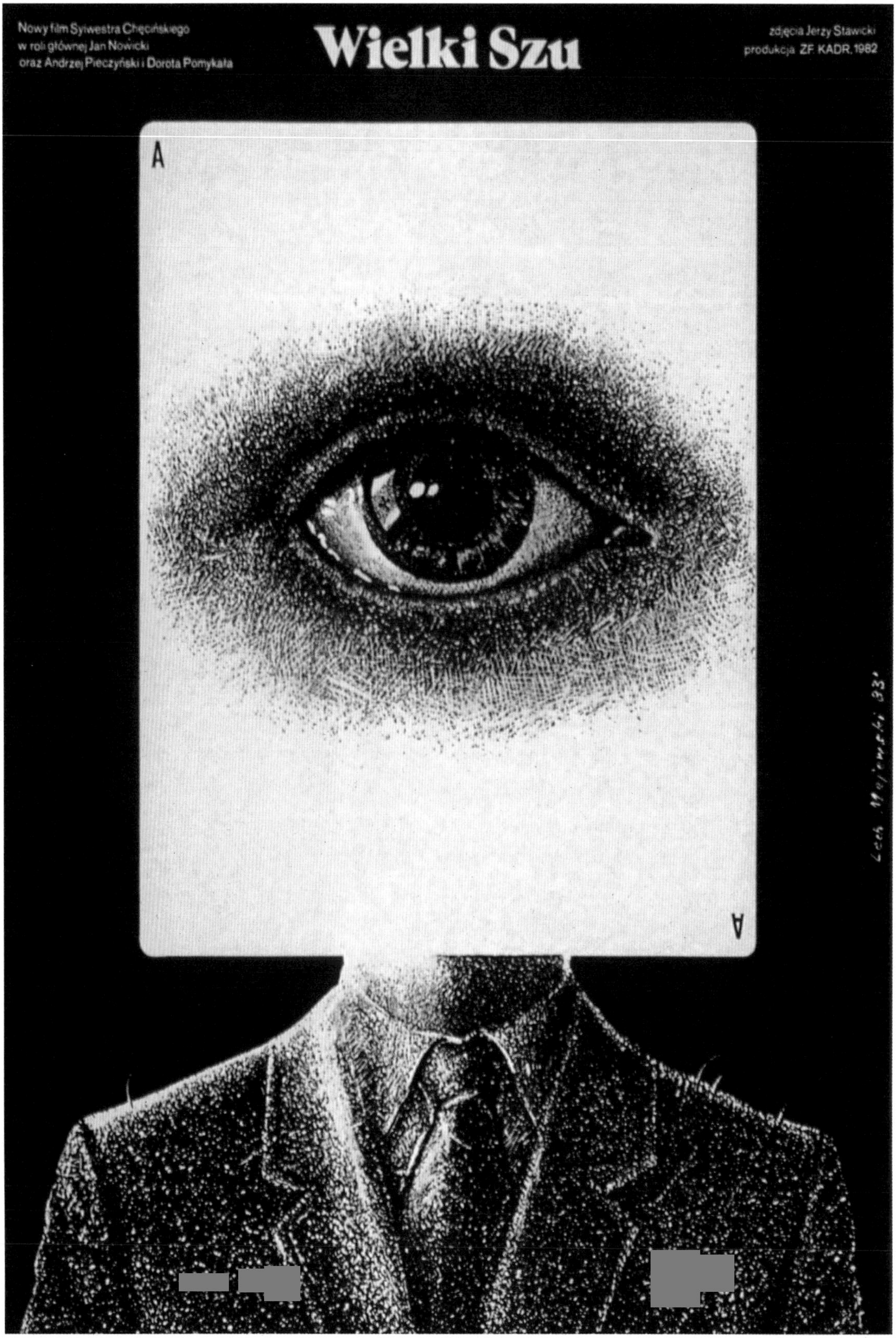

« Big Shar ». Poster. 1983. 98 x 68 cm. Offset. Client: ZRF. Poster for a polish film.

« Uninteresting Story ». Poster. 1983. 98 x 68 cm. Offset. Client: ZRF. Poster for a polish film.

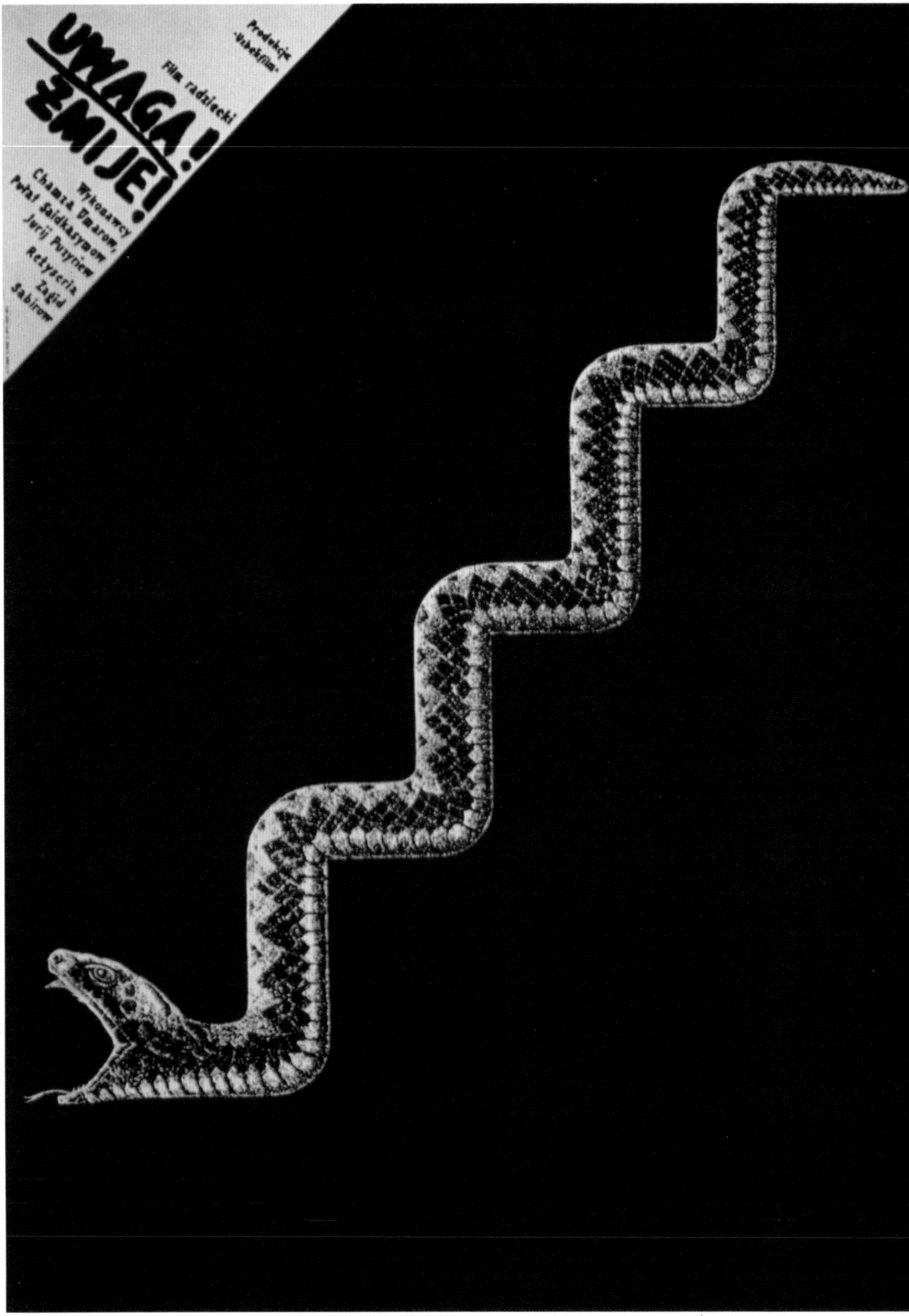

« Attention Vipers ». Film Poster. 1981. 98 x 68 cm. Offset. Client: CWF.

« Adam Majak. Sculptur». Poster. 2005. 98 x 68 cm. Client: Zacheta.

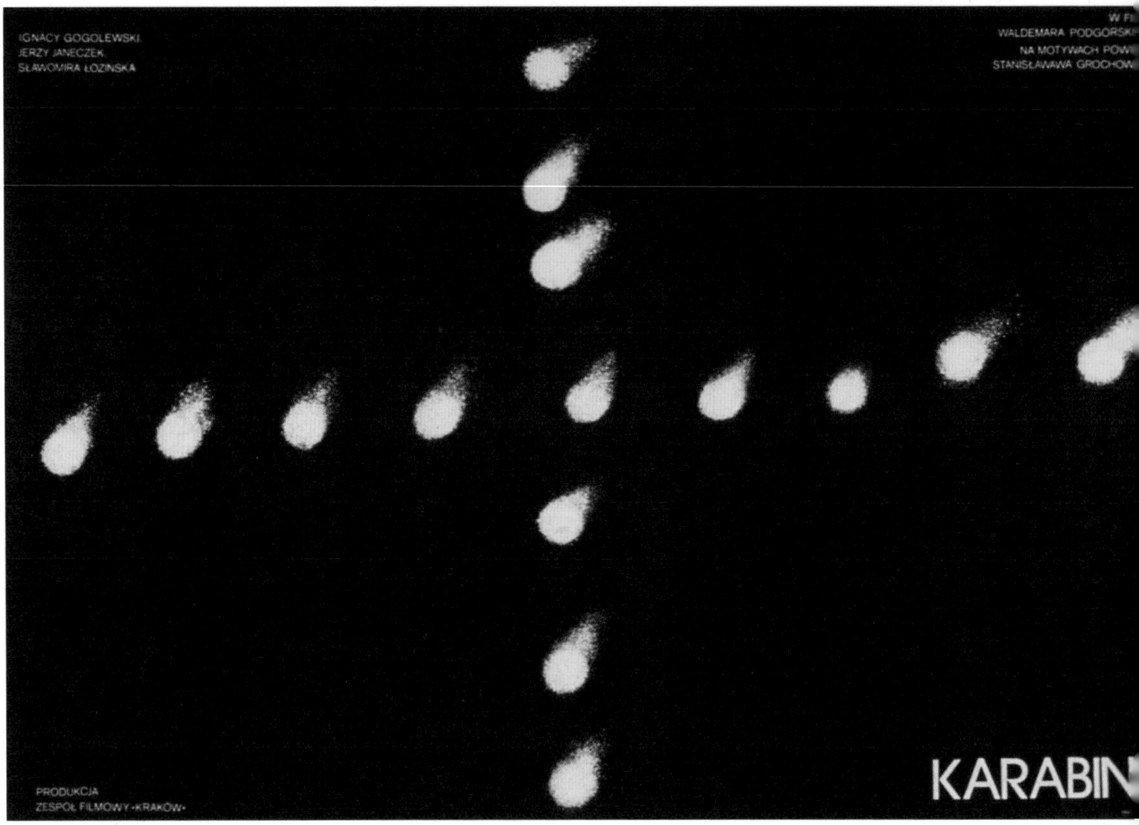

« Rifles 1 » . Poster. 1982. 68 x 98 cm. Offset. Client: Polfilm. Poster for a film

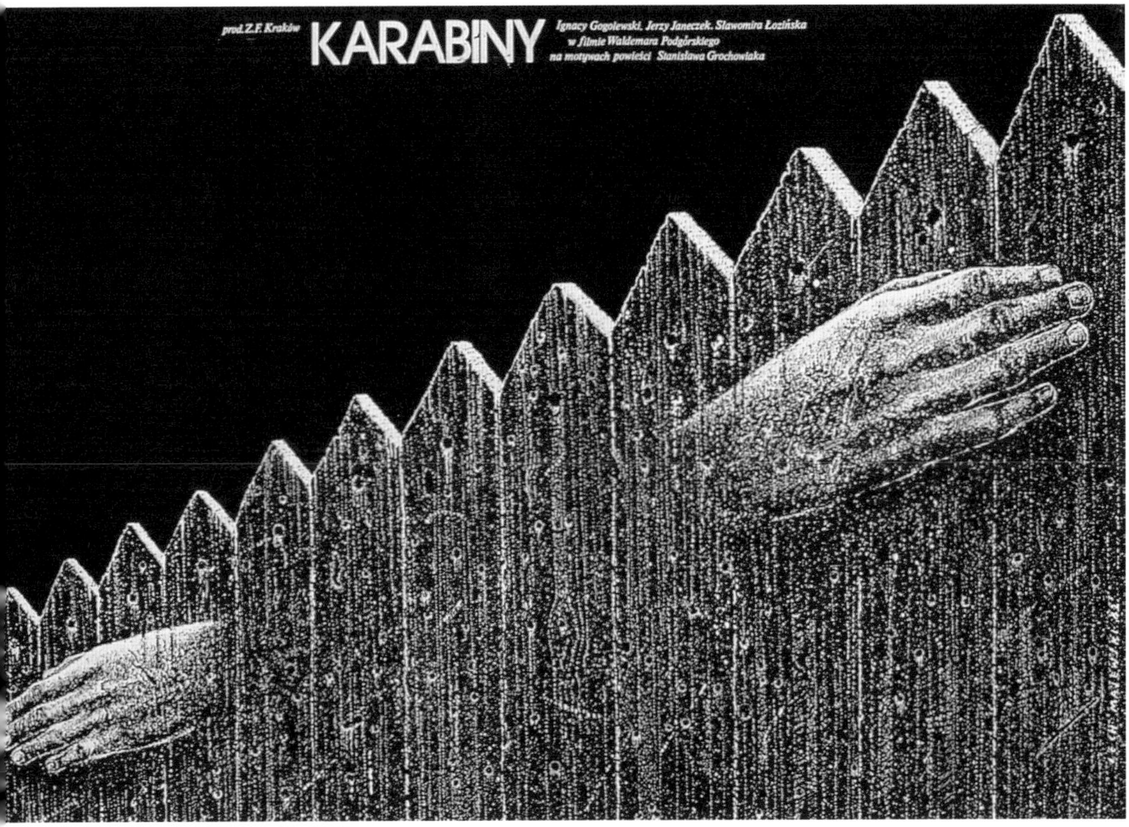

« Rifles 2 » . Poster. 1982. 68 x 98 cm. Offset. Client: Polfilm. Poster for a film.

« Chain » 1981, 68 x 98 cm, Offset. Client: CRF. Poster for a polish film.

« Mont of Memory ». 1983, 68 x 98 cm. Offset. Client: KAW.

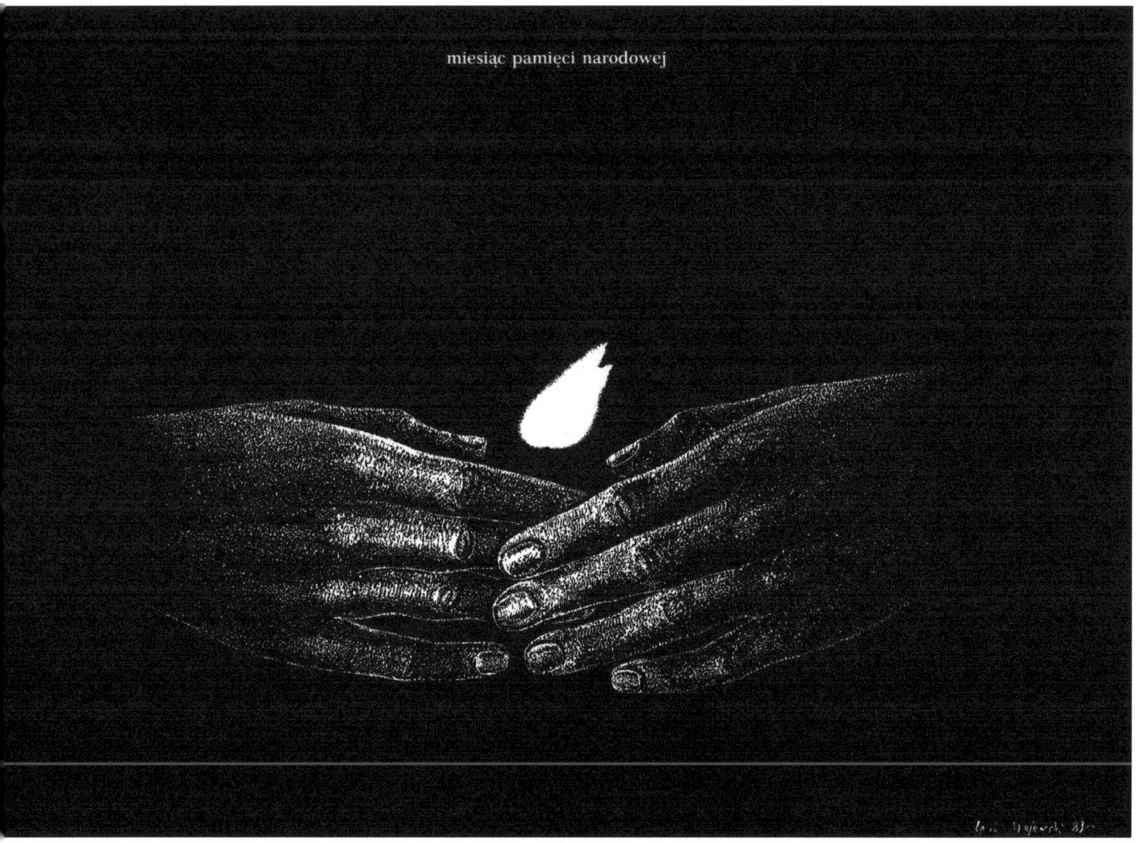

Lech Majewski's Poster by Wang Xu

Wojciech Fangor said in 1957 that, "From the viewpoint of film circulation in Poland, film posters are practically useless." I wonder if the artist was aware how prophetic he was about the origin of the Polish School of Poster Design. This unique phenomenon consisted in the divorce of the artistic function (of posters in general, not just film posters) from commercial considerations and a draughtsman's discipline, and shifting poster design towards genuine art.

"Visual metaphor", "graphic aphorism", and "depicted illusion" were the signposts along this route. I am calling all this for the sake of the younger readers who did not witness the birth of the new trend. Only those aware of it may appreciate the role of intellectual design and metaphor in the works of Lech Majewski. It would be very difficult to decide whether apart from the information they contain they advertise films, theater productions or jazz concerts in the classical sense of the word "advertisement". Rather, they look like prints inspired by the cultural events behind them: they are artistic "impressions on the subject" rather than descriptions. One of the significant qualities of Majewski's art has to do with the spectator and his perception. We are interested in the graphic message conveyed by his posters; not only before but also (or primarily) after seeing a film or a play, wanting to compare our feelings and associations with those of the designer. When he designs film or theater posters (which he likes doing best), he carefully follows their plots, anxious as he says to arrive at his own visual code, faithful to the director's concept, but without imitating it. This is his first statement in his dialogue with the viewer's imagination. Rather than saying "go to the cinema", he prefers to intrigue the cinemagoer, Majewski's posters are situated half way between the two extremes of contemporary poster design. One borders on painting permeated with literary not to say fictional qualities, the other seeks for a crisp sign adding point to the work recommended. Majewski's film posters like the Racing Stable Manager, 'A Flush of Feeling' or 'Under the Volcano' are closer to the former tendency; his works Ceramics for Architecture, Attention! Vipers! and the Guns in the original version, are based on graphic abbreviation. A large majority of Majewski's works represent the happy mean, which is where he feels at his best. He say that he enjoys himself when designing posters.

« The scent of dog's fur ». Sketches for the poster. 1982.

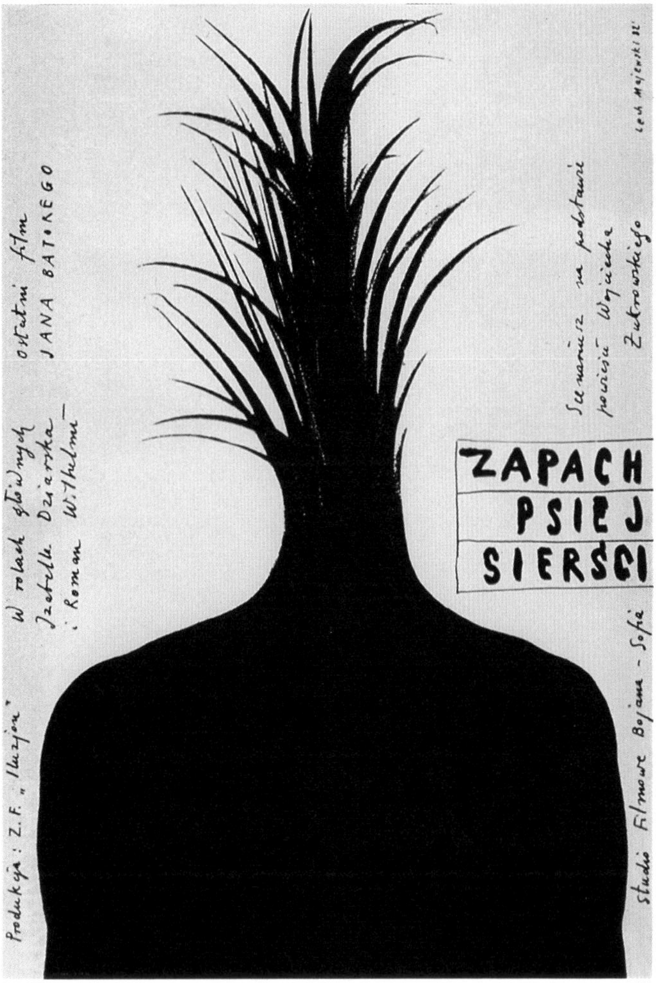

« The scent of dog's fur ». Poster. 1982. 98 x 68 cm. Offset. Client: Polfilm.

This is why now, at his mature stage, he does not over-exploit conventions or ideas worked out in the past. He uses them once, and at most repeats them in a different form in later works (as in A Tedious Story and Chain, or Under the Volcano and Girl Rogues). Then he abandons them to give room for new associations so that the public looks forward to seeing the development of his work (see the accompanying reproductions).

It is clear that a changing color, used without striking contrasts, is not an isolated, superior value on which the ultimate impact of his posters depends, as is the case with many outstanding colorists in Polish poster design. It corresponds to what Majewski says of his style: It is uniform because of the intellectual attitude towards the subject rather than formal similarities". To me, Majewski's best works are in black and white, e.g. The Smell of a Dog's Fur, Attentions! Vipers!
or Dupont Lajoie. The latter poster is the epitome of my favorite style, a combination of the trends mentioned before, adding up to what I call "Majewski's literature of signs".

"The New Edition of Design Exchange no.12", China Youth

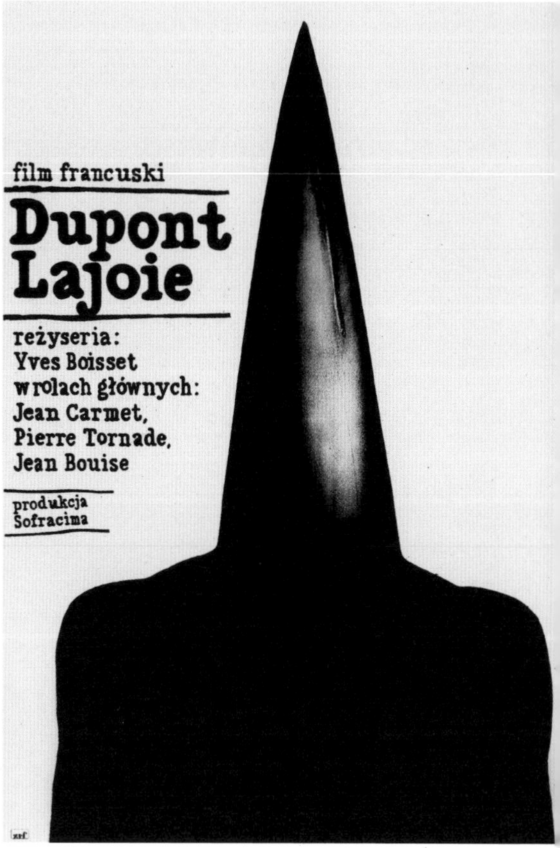

« Gli Ordini Sono Ordini ». 1974. Film Poster. 84 x 60 cm. Offset. Client: CWE.
« Dupont lajoie ». Poster. 1977. 98 x 68 cm. Offset. Client: ZRF. Poster for a french film

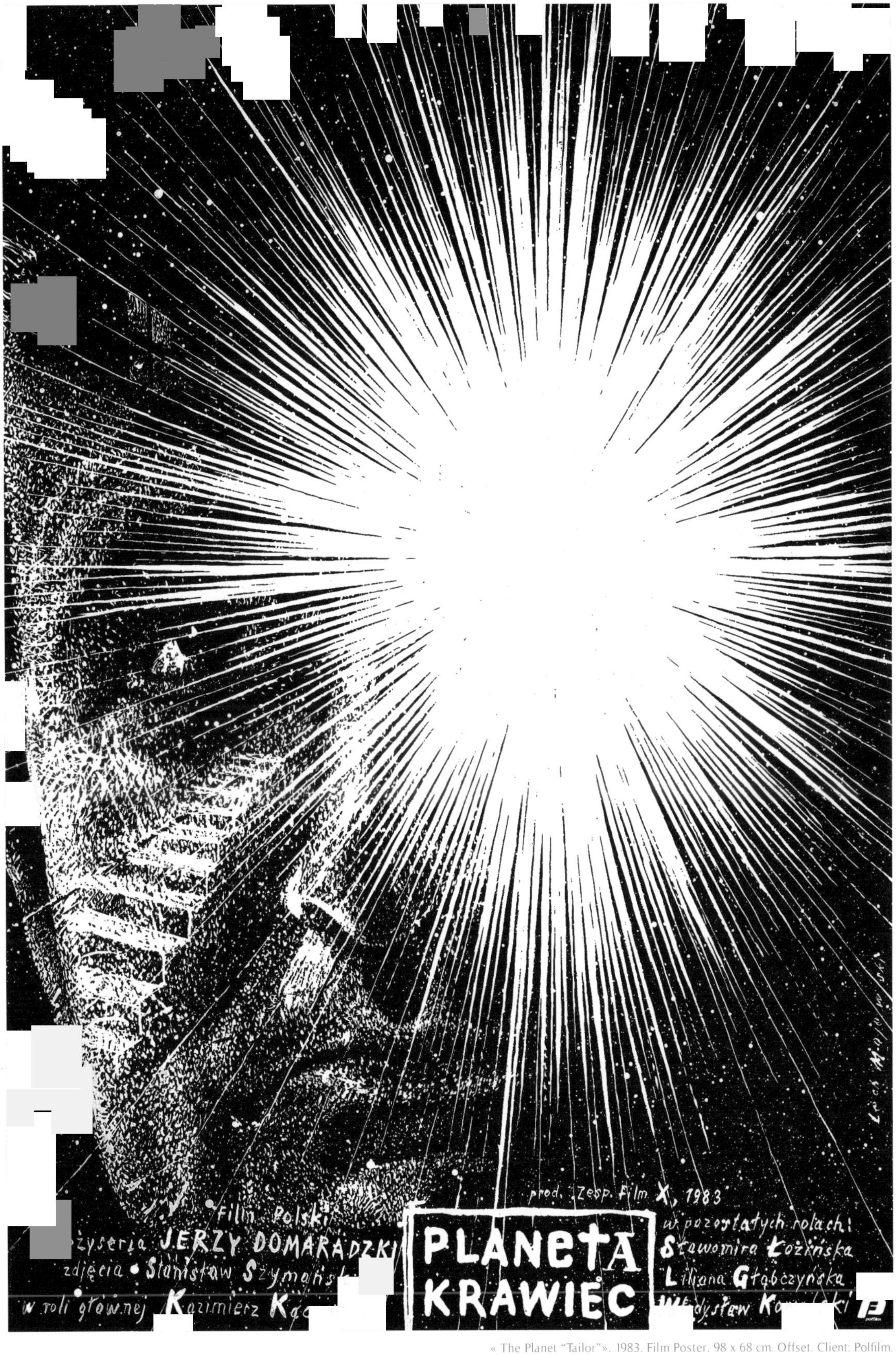

« The Planet "Tailor"». 1983. Film Poster. 98 x 68 cm. Offset. Client: Polfilm.

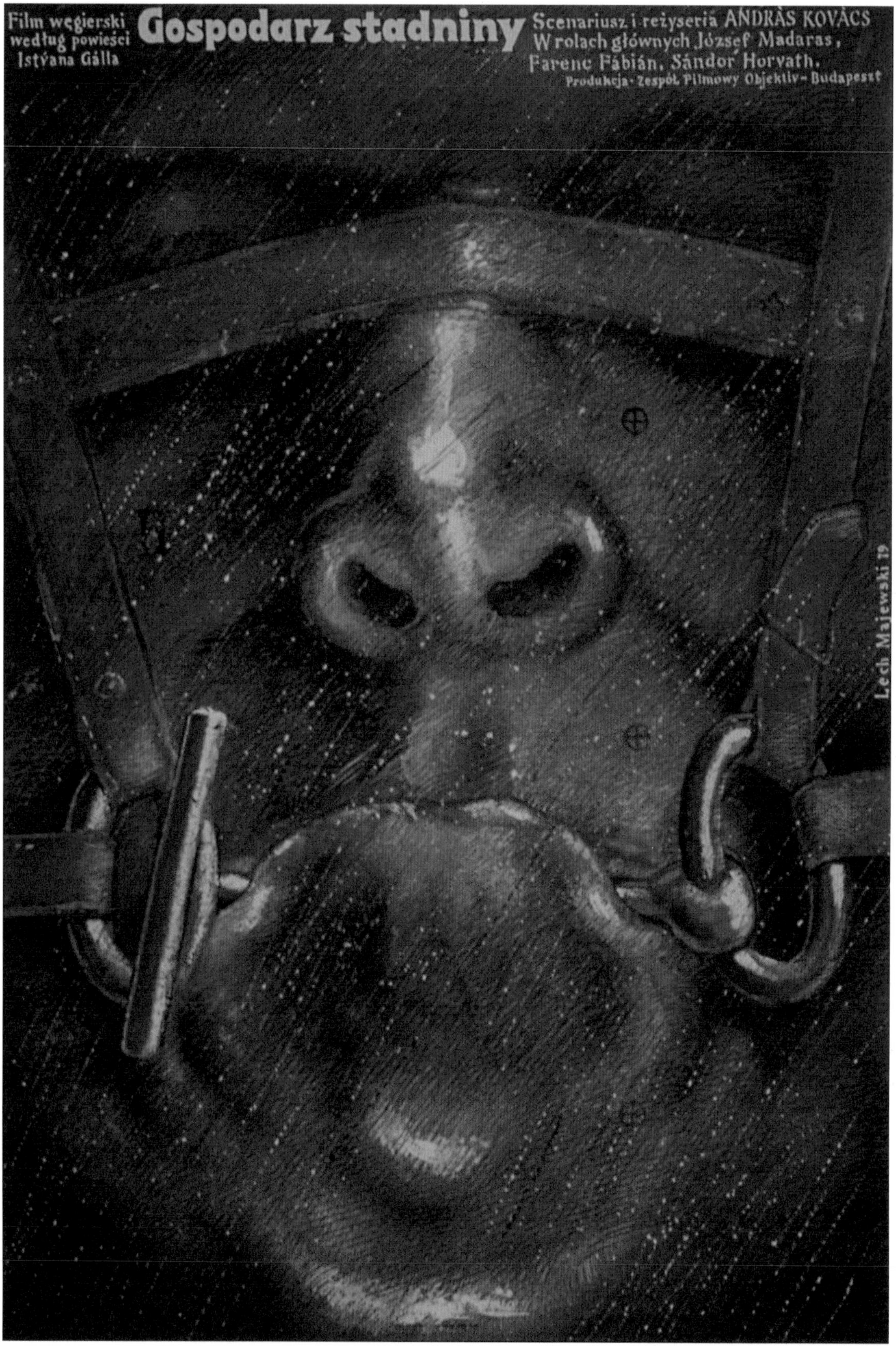

« Lord of the Stud ». Poster. 1979. 98 x 68 cm. Offset. Client: CRF. Poster for a hungarian film.

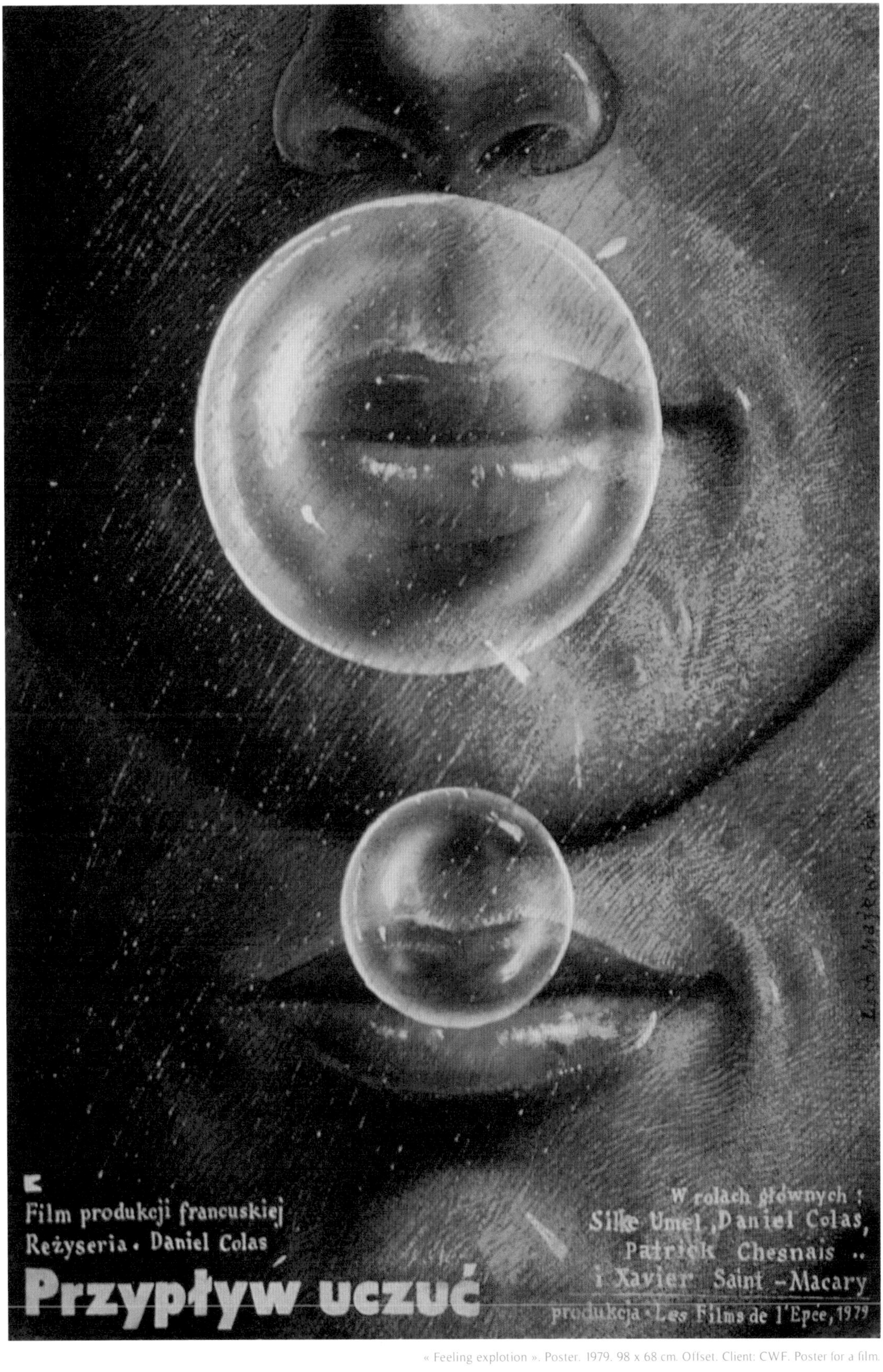

« Feeling explotion ». Poster. 1979. 98 x 68 cm. Offset. Client: CWF. Poster for a film.

« Passenger ». Poster. 1984. 68 x 98 cm. Offset. Client: ZRF. Poster for a chinese film.

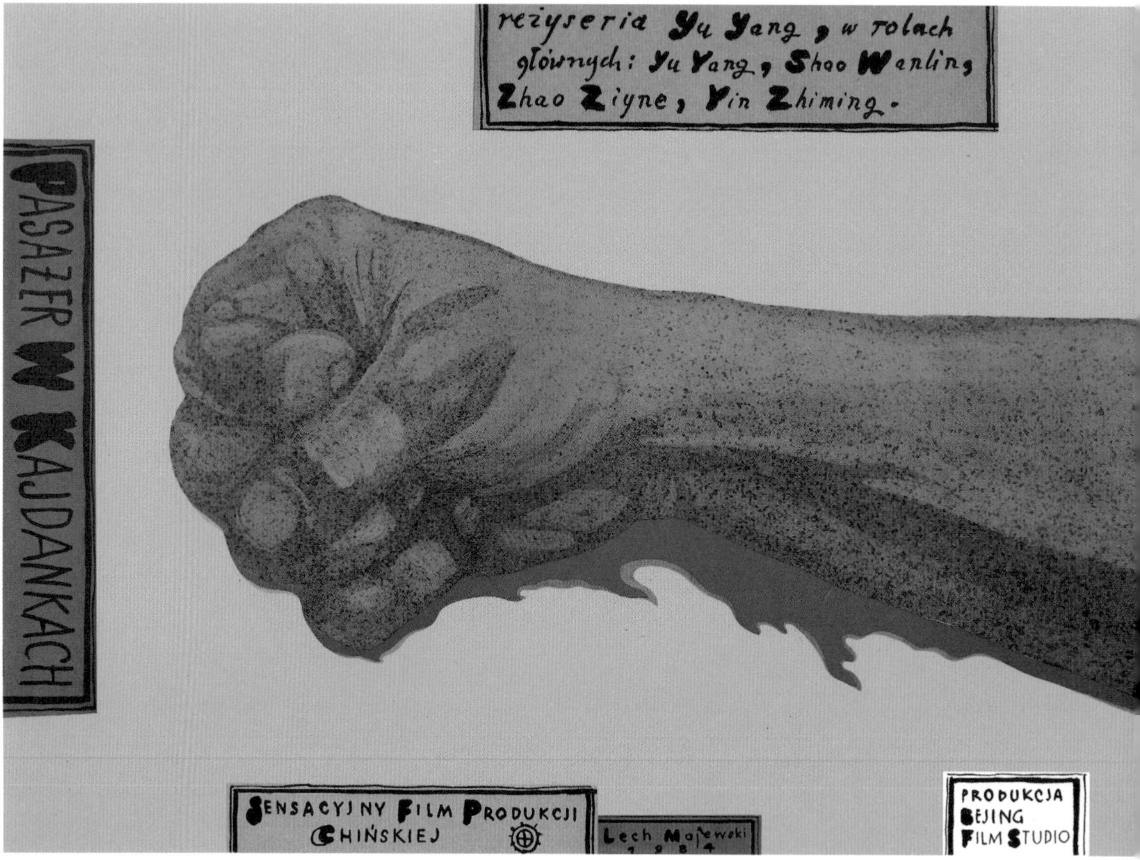

« Temporary Release ». Poster. 1980. 68 x 98 cm. Offset. Client: CWF. Poster for an american film.

ZWOLNIENIE WARUNKOWE
Lech Majewski M 1980
Film produkcji USA · Reżyseria Ulu Grosbard
Adaptacja powieści · Edwarda Bunkera
• W rolach głównych: DUSTIN HOFFMAN,
Theresa Russel, Gary Busey, Harry Dean Stanton
Produkcja: A Sweet Wall Production - 1978

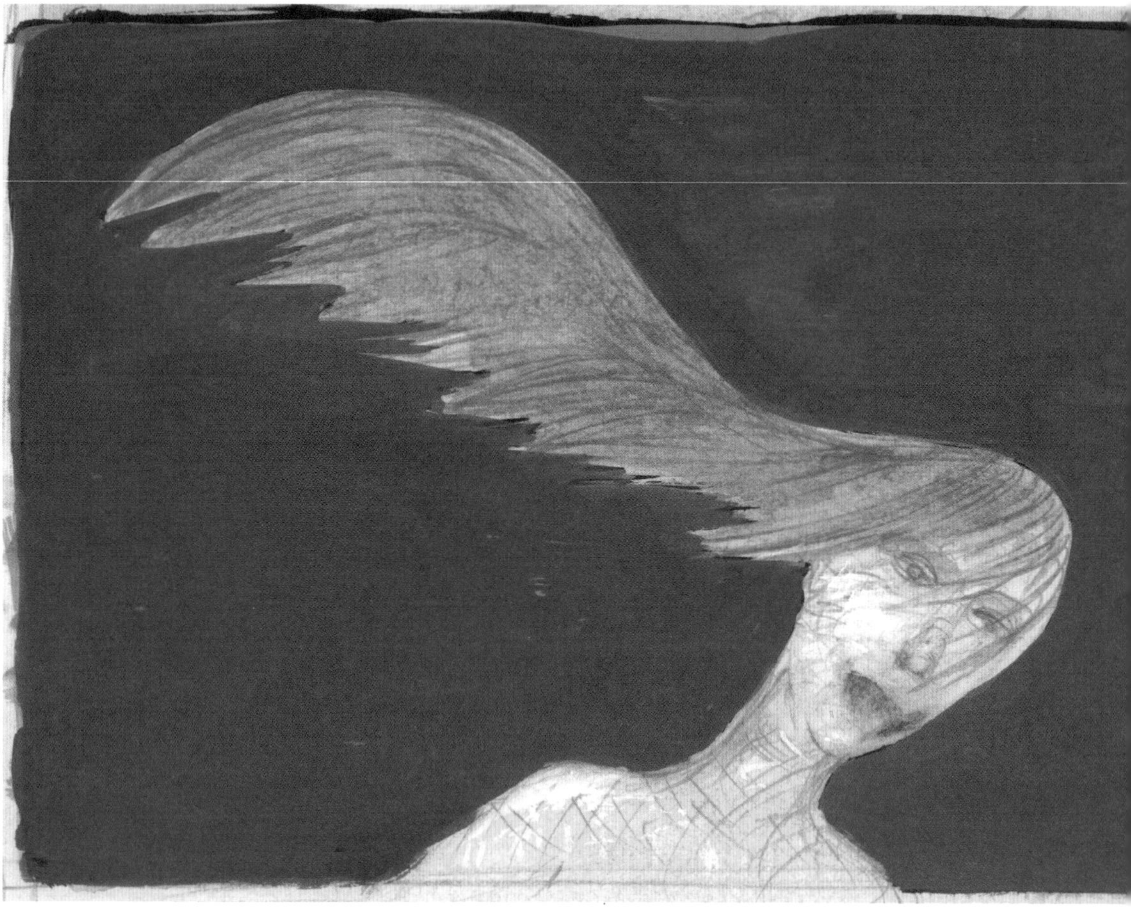

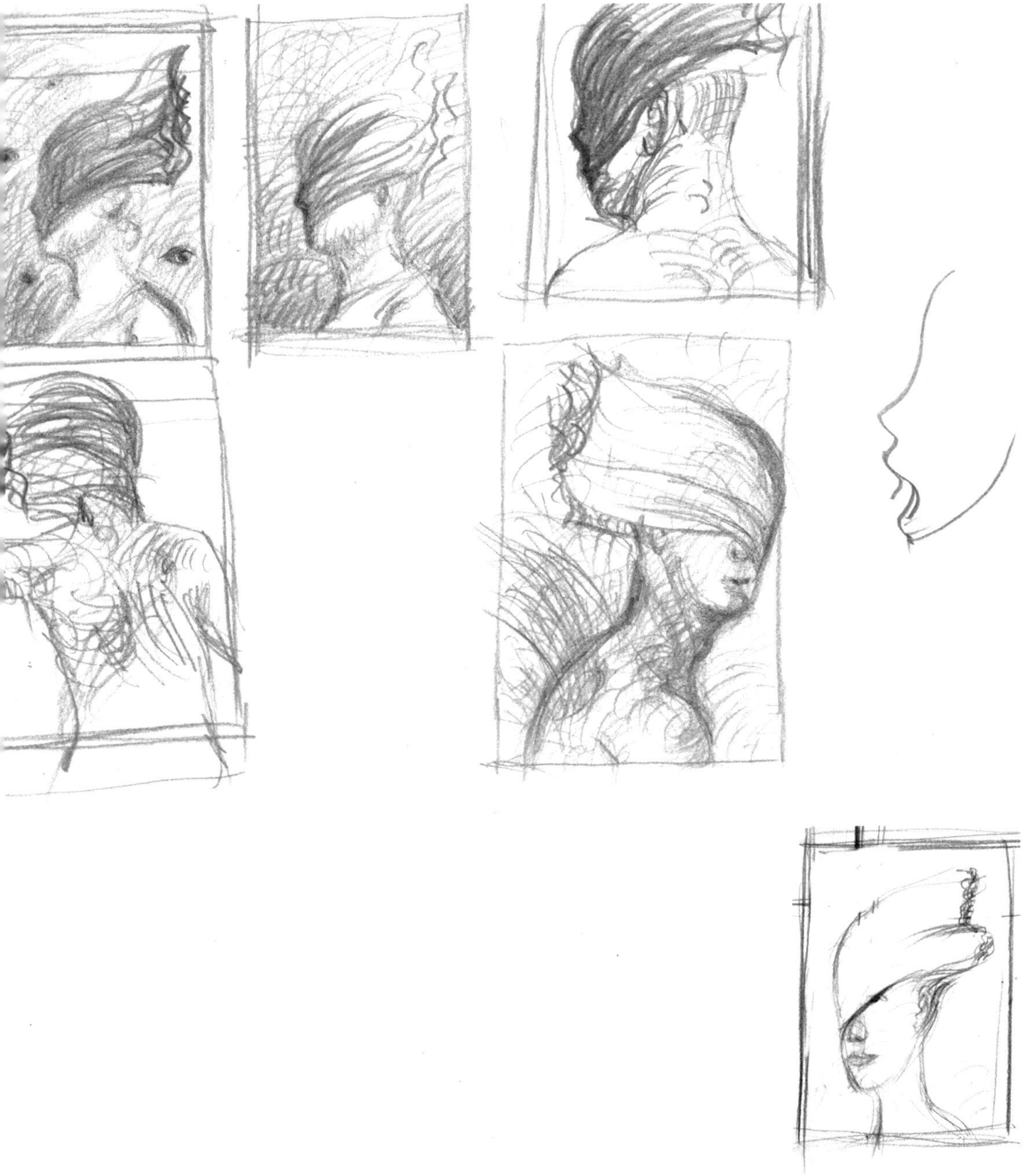

« Under Volcano ». Sketches for the poster. 1984.

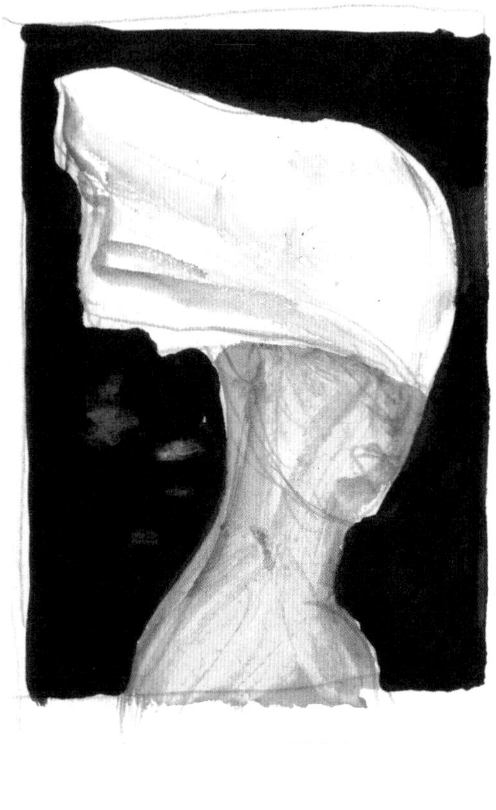

« Under Volcano ». Sketches for the poster. 1984.

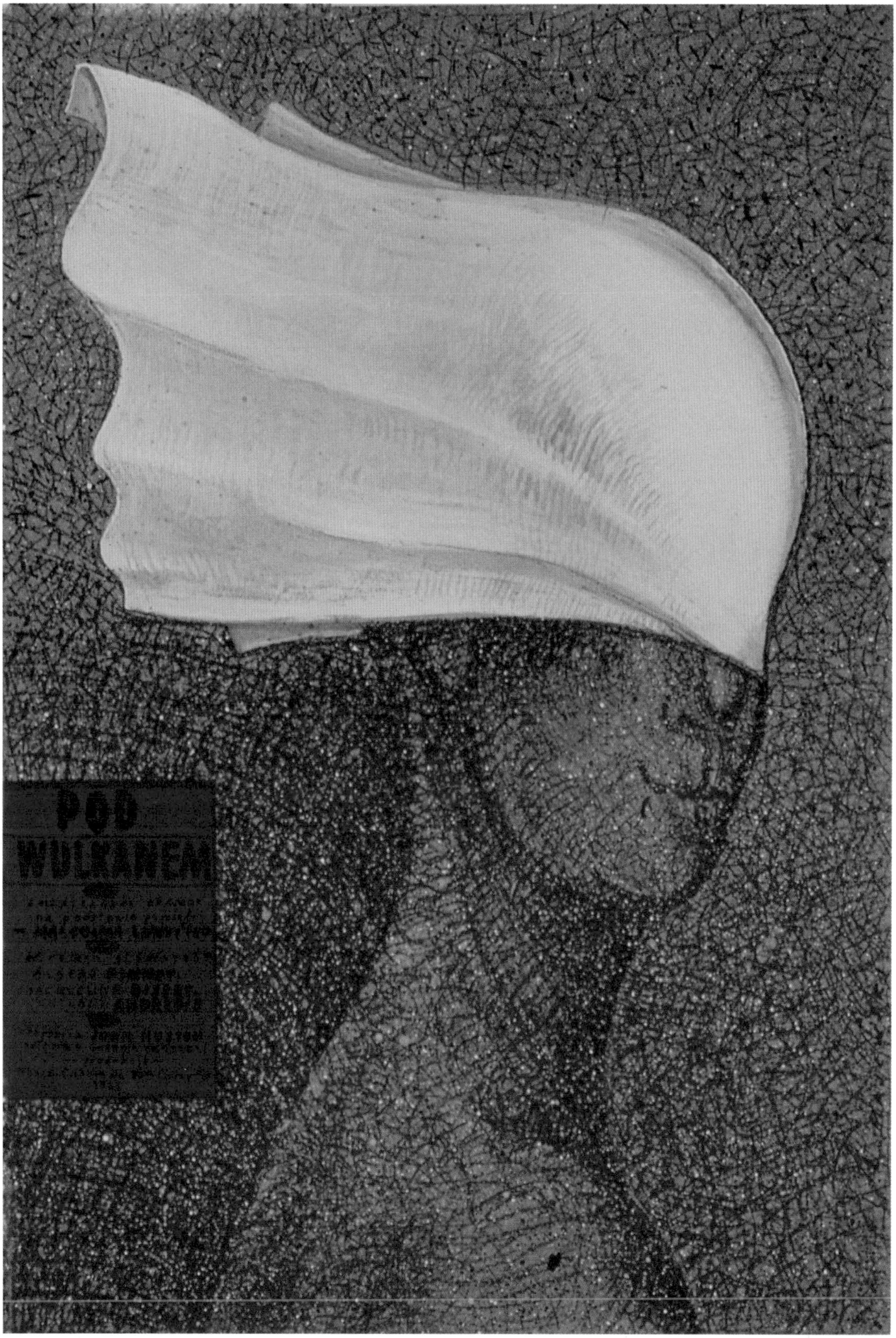

« Under Volcano ». Poster. 1984. 98 x 68 cm. Offset. Client: CWF.

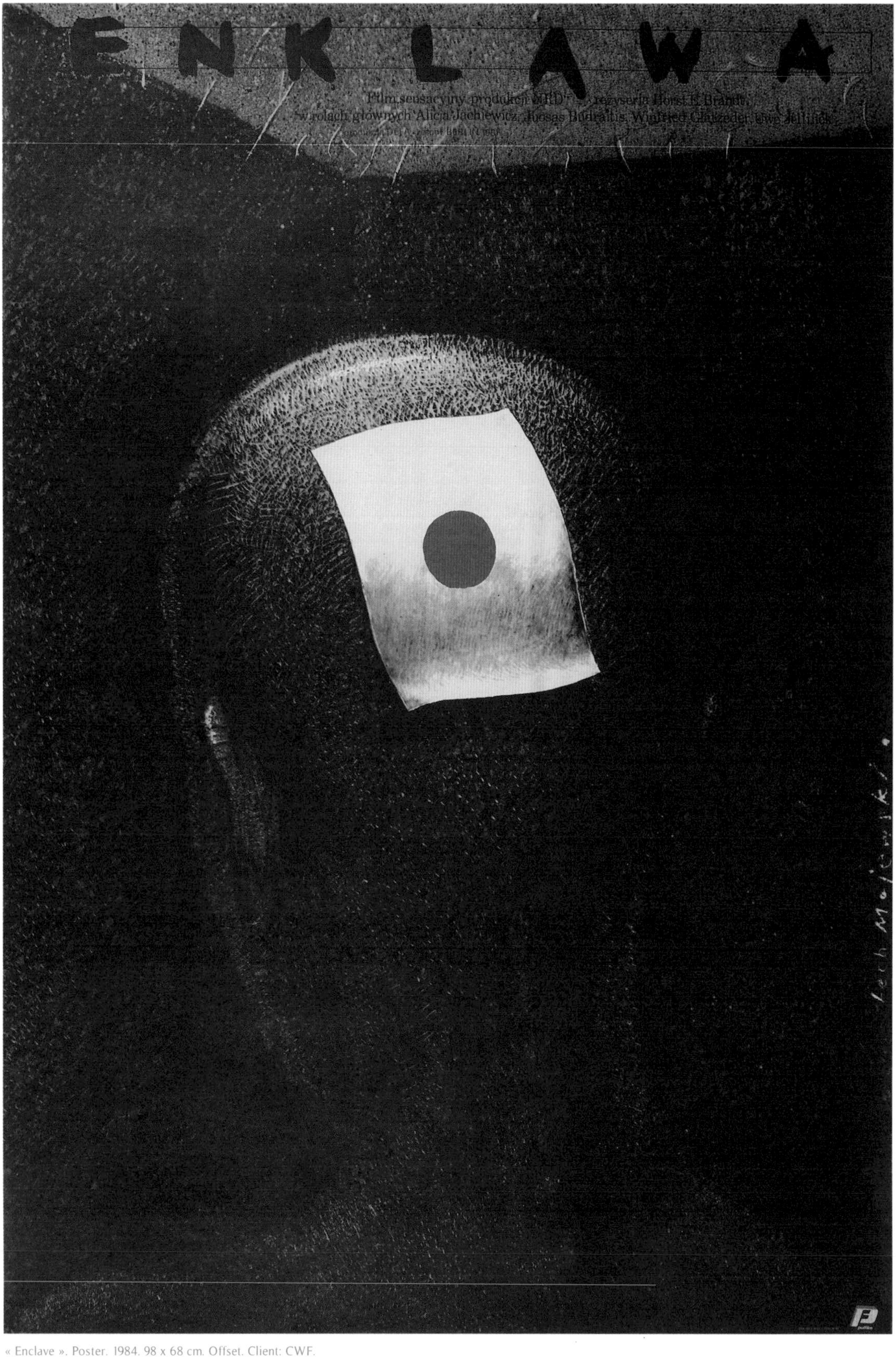

« Enclave ». Poster. 1984. 98 x 68 cm. Offset. Client: CWF.

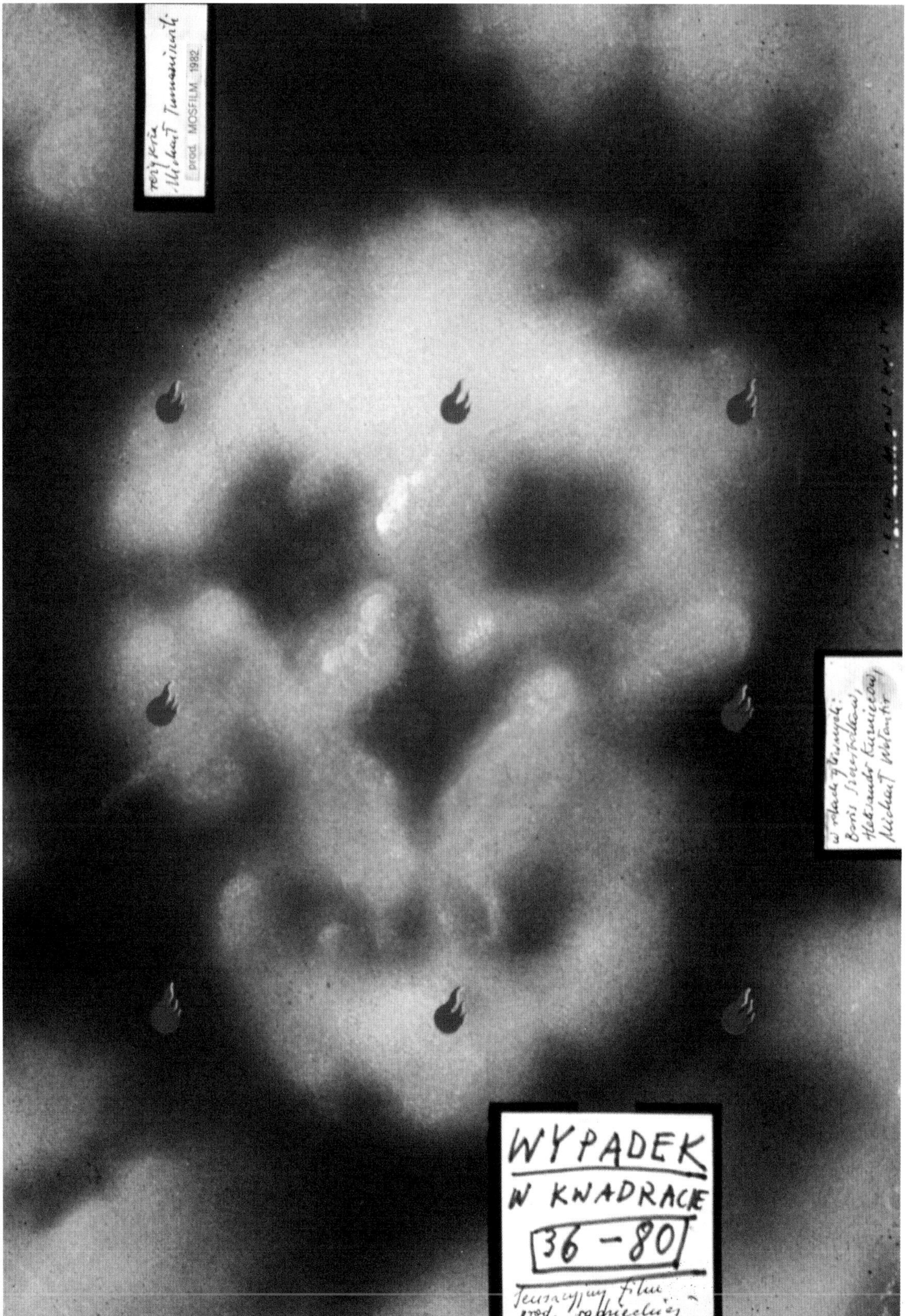

« Incident at Map-Grid 36-80 ». Poster. 1986. 98 x 68 cm. Offset. Client: CRF.

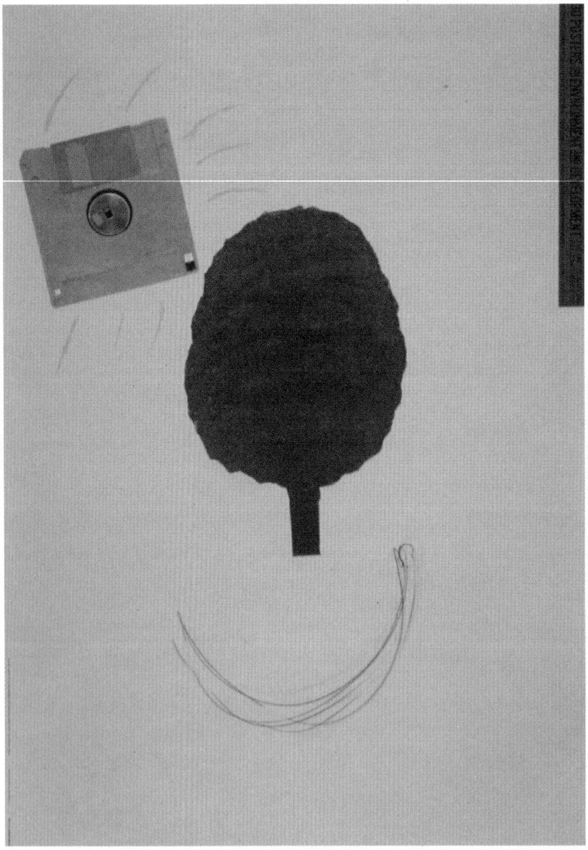

« Environment and Developement ». Poster. 1992. 70 x 50 cm. Offset. Client: Eco Conference in Rio Janeiro.
« The Vistula River in Modern Art ». Poster. 1985. 98 x 68 cm. Offset. Client: KAW.

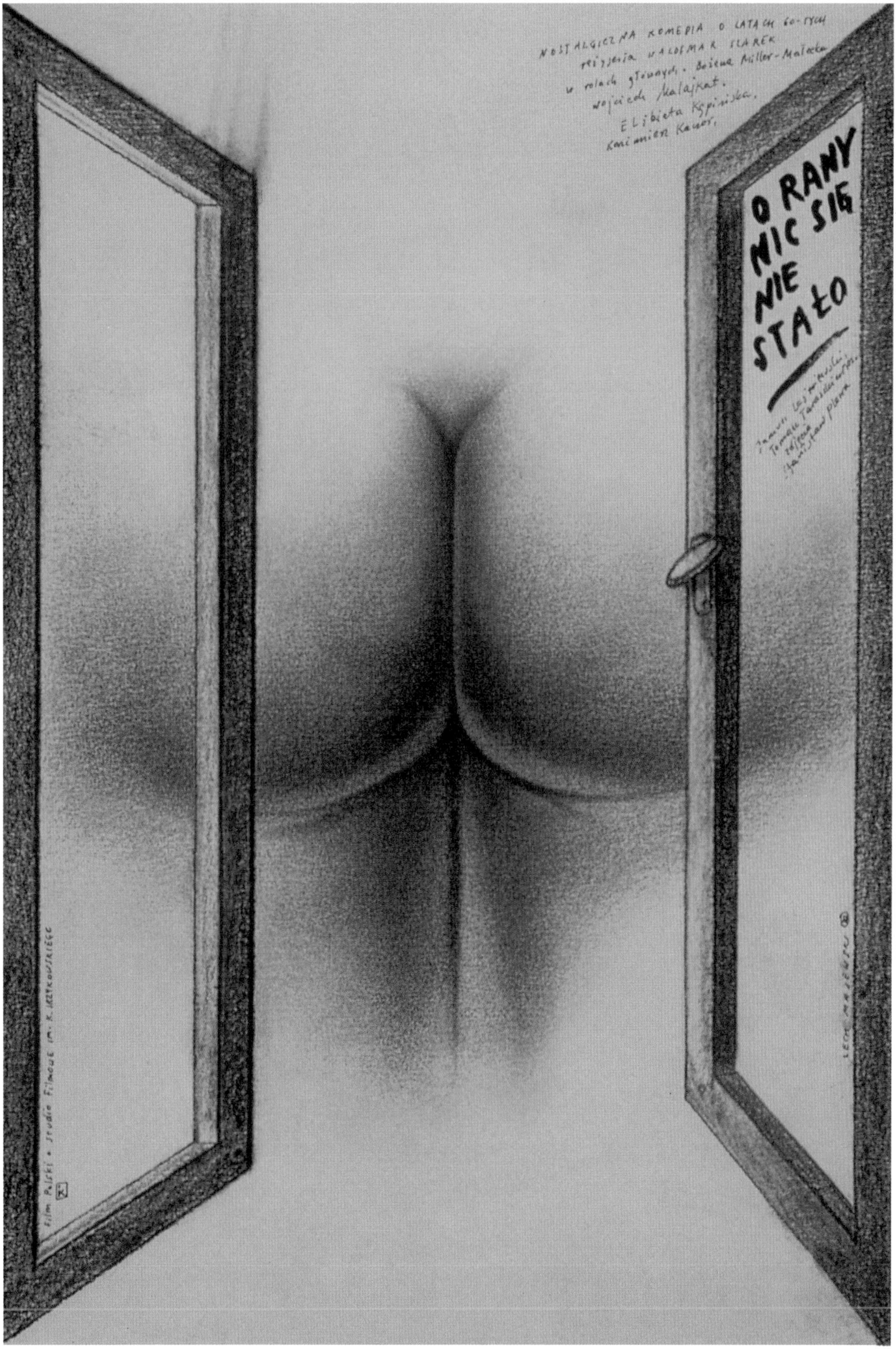

« O rany, nic sie nie stalo ». Poster. 1988. 98 x 68 cm. Offset. Client: Polfilm.

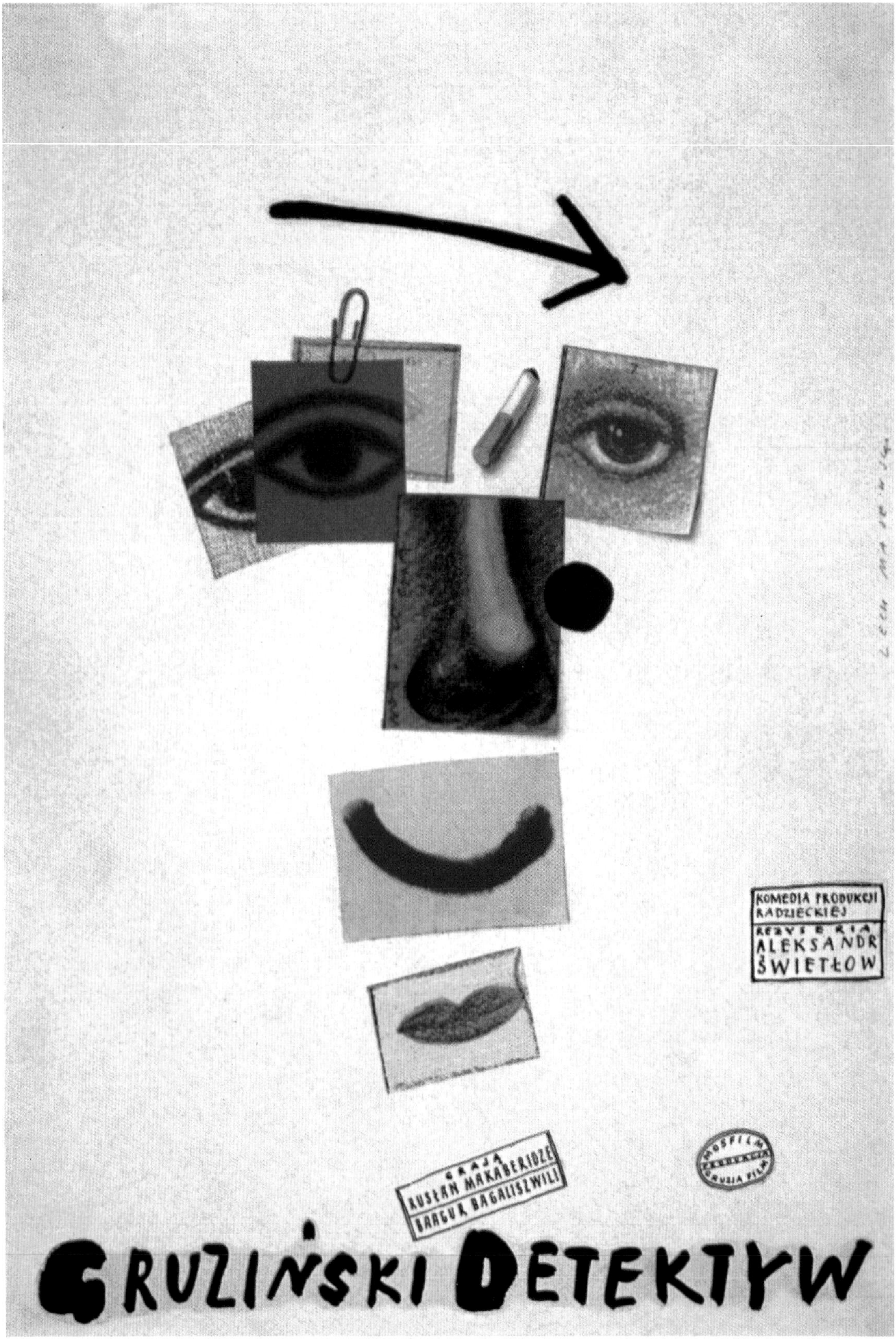

« Georgian detective ». Poster. 1990. 98 x 68 cm. Offset. Client: ZRF.

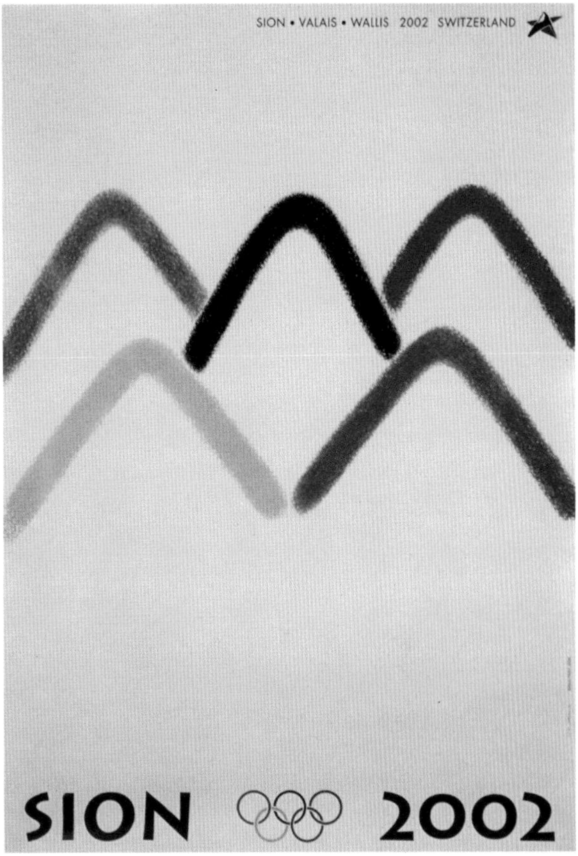

« European Juniors Championships in Canoeing ». Poster. 1972. 98 x 68 cm. Offset. Client: KAW.
« SION 2002 ». Poster. 2001. 198 x 168 cm. Offset. Client: Swiss Olympic Committee.

« Untitled ». Drawing.

« Ballet ». Poster. 1989. 98 x 68 cm. Offset. Client: Teatr Wielki in Warsaw.

LECH MAJEWSKI JULISTEITA POSTERS
GALLERIA TÄYSIKUU 6.3 –26. 3. 91
AVOINNA • MA – SULJ.
TI–PE 14-20 • LA 10–16 • SU 12–18
LINJA -AUTOASEMA, EROTTAJA 1, 96100 ROVANIEMI, PUH 322 2236 • KULTTUURITOIMISTO

« Lech Wajewski's Poster Exhibition in Rovaniemi in Finnland ». Poster. 1991. 100 x 70 cm. Silk screen. Client: Galleria Täysikuu.

« Lech Majewski Posters, exhibition in Zamosc ». Poster. 1992. 70 x 70 cm. Offset. Client: WDK.

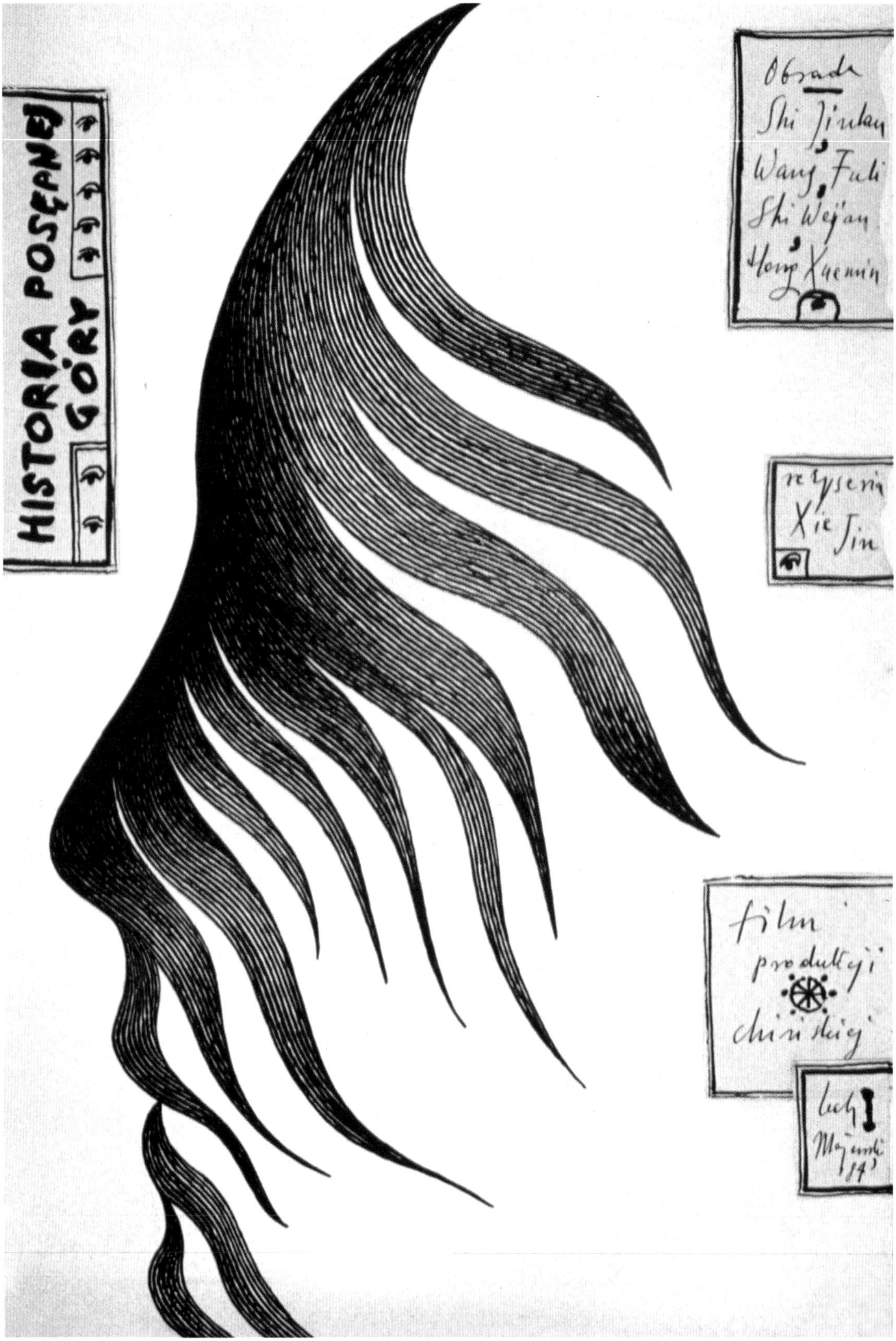

« Story of dark montain ». Film poster. 1984. 98 x 68 cm. Offset. Client: CWF.

A Case of an Artistic Transformation by Peter Gyllan

One of the grooviest and most surprising contributions I received when editing a book on international poster art, recently, were the works sent by the Pole, Lech Majewski. Surprising, because it is seldom that such an established designer is able to reinvent the means of his graphic expression the way this art academy professor from Warsaw has done. The mere mention of the Polish capital in the context of posters gives most of our "graphic minds", immediate associations to the city's first and foremost international poster biennial. If picturing the busy body Lech Majewski comes next, it is understandable, as he has been involved in the biennial's organizing committe, ever since the late 80's. As well as presiding over it since 1994, so there is no doubt about it: Lech is a man of action!

His own exhibition début took place with a couple of posters (which he positively would not want to be reminded of) exactly thirty years ago, at the 5th Biennale of 1974. Three biennials later, he received an honorary prize – the first in a row of distinctions, which include the ICOGRADA Award at the Trnava Poster Triennial 2003.

As exceptional as his 1982 film poster "The Smell of the Dog's Fur" happened to be, for the following decade, Lech was just one of a dozen solid representatives of the Polish poster's so-called "second post-war generation". A wave that followed "the invasion of the giants" – Cieslewicz, Gorka, Lenica, Mlodozeniec, Starowieyski, Swierzy, Urbaniec, as well as the professor's professor, Henryk Tomaszewski. This is history, of course, while the reason behind this presentation of Lech Majewski to the readers of Novum is the novelty of his recent production. These works strike me as being both original in their own right, and different from any earlier design coming from the man's atelier.

The spirit of the sophisticated simplicity, typical of his master's - Henryk Tomaszewski's posters – is now pronounced more than ever, but it has been twisted into a kind of a colourful theatrical imagery featuring stupefying typographic elements, equal in their share of post-modernism and native folklore.

Majewski is a highly valued educator (see: Novum 09/03 for examples of his students' works). On the Warsaw's Art Academy's website, he deliberates the issue of the impact the radical changes in media and technology is having on contemporary visual communication. Judging from the inventiveness of "Bal", "Kolendziolki" and the rest of the Rzeszow Theatre series, it certainly appears to have had a remarkable effect on the transformation of his own poster design.

Novum Plus (07/2004): Posters / Lech Majewski (PL)

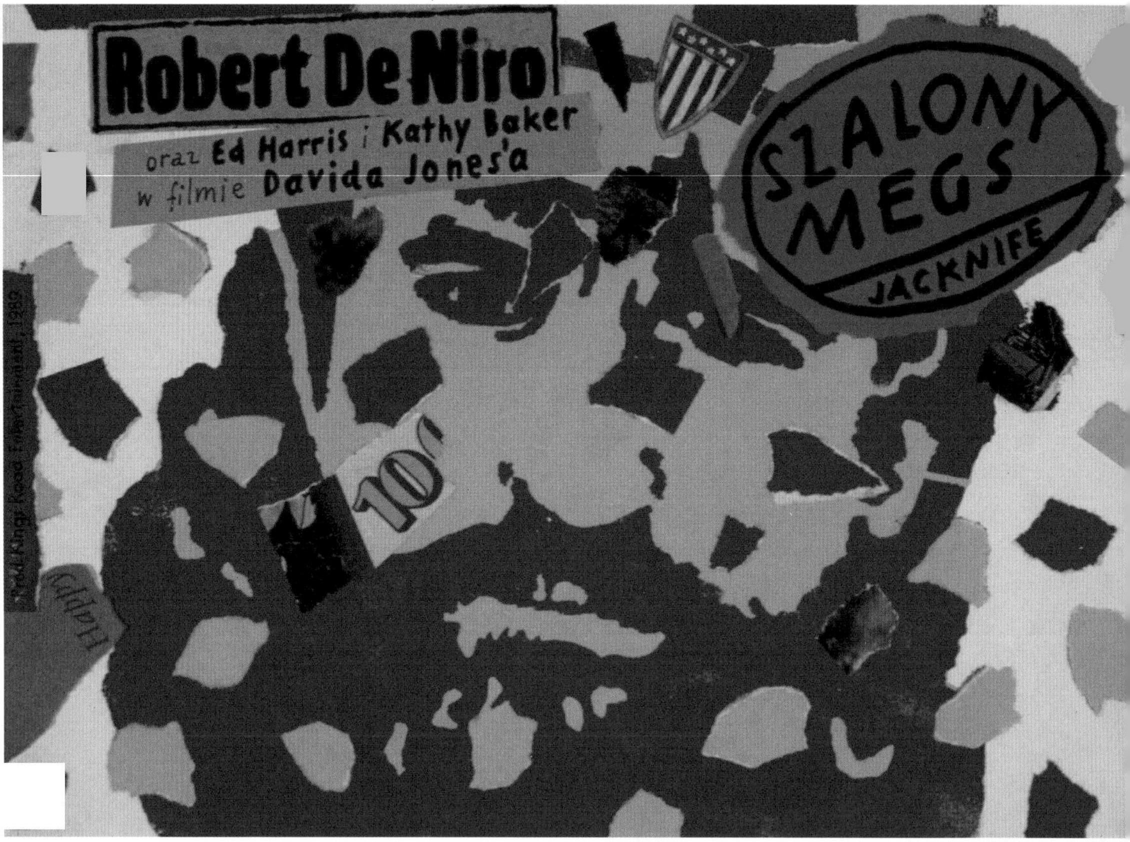

Left: « Jacknife ». Poster. 1989. 68 x 98 cm. Offset. Client: ZRF
Right: « Safe holiday with Toyota ». Poster. 2002. 68 x 98 cm. Offset. Client: Toyota Motor Poland.
Under: « Untitled ». Drawing.

Bezpieczne wakacje z Toyotą
TOYOTA
TOYOTA MOTOR POLAND

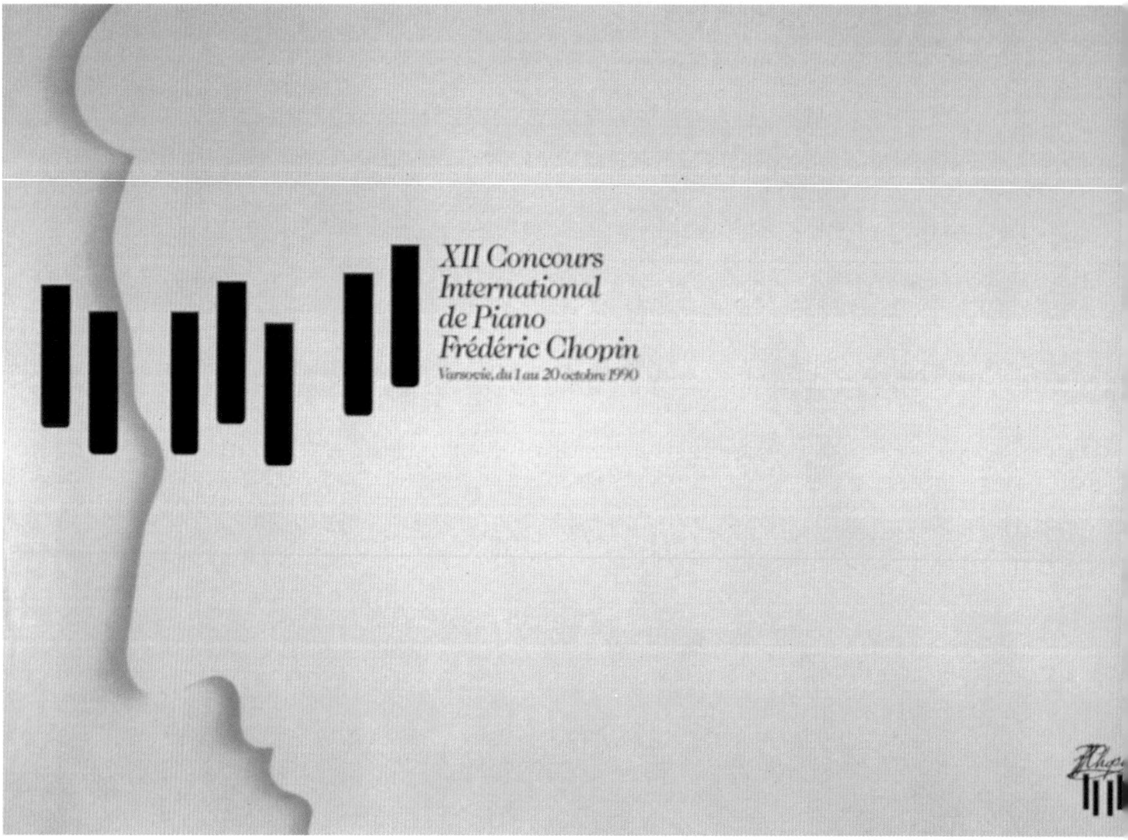
XII Concours
International
de Piano
Frédéric Chopin
Varsovie, du 1 au 20 octobre 1990

Left above: « The International Frederick Chopin Piano Competition » Poster. 1990. 68 x 98 cm. Offset. Client: KAW.
Left under: « Untitled ». Drawing. Right above: « Congress of the Polish Culture ». Poster. 1981. 68 x 98 cm.

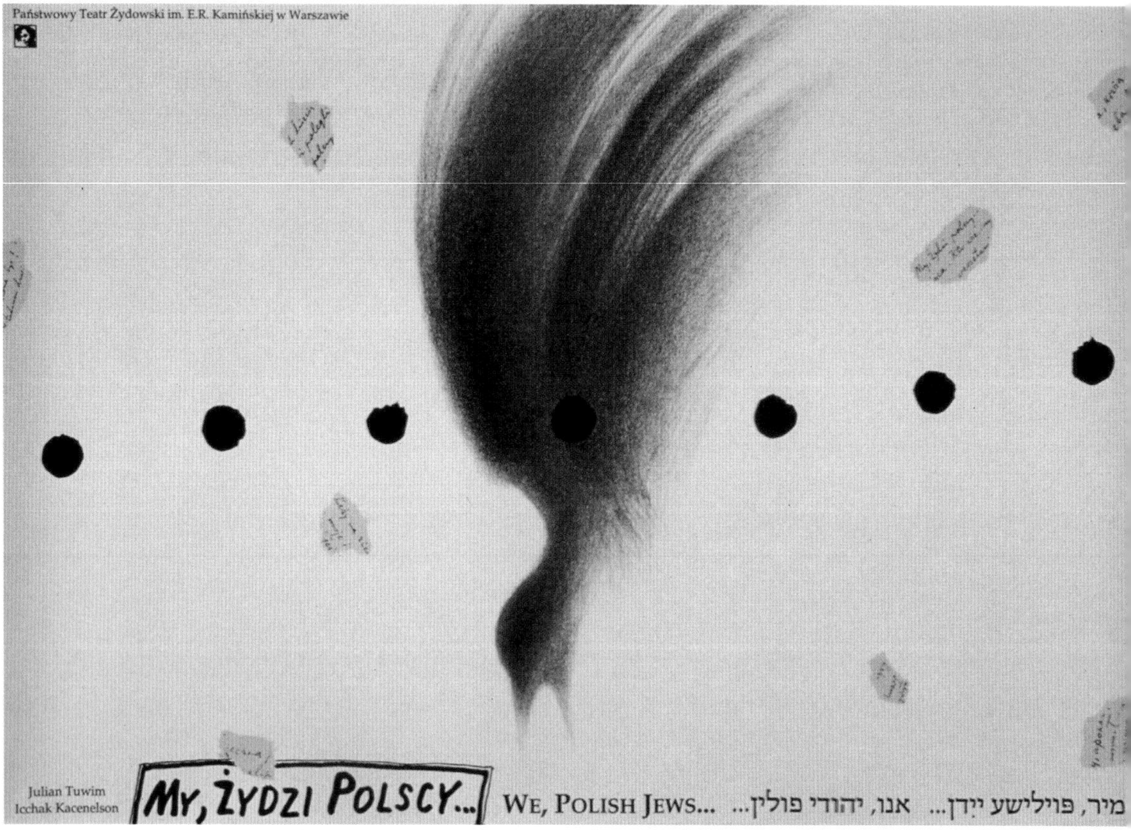
Państwowy Teatr Żydowski im. E.R. Kamińskiej w Warszawie
Julian Tuwim
Icchak Kacenelson
MY, ŻYDZI POLSCY...
WE, POLISH JEWS...
...אנו, יהודי פולין
...מיר, פוילישע יידן

Left: « We, Polish Jewsh ». Poster. 68 x 98 cm. Offset. Client: Poster Jewish Theatre in Warsaw.
Right: « 200 years of French Revolution ». Poster. 68 x 98 cm. Offset. Client: Poster Museum in Warsaw.
Under: « Untitled ». Drawing.

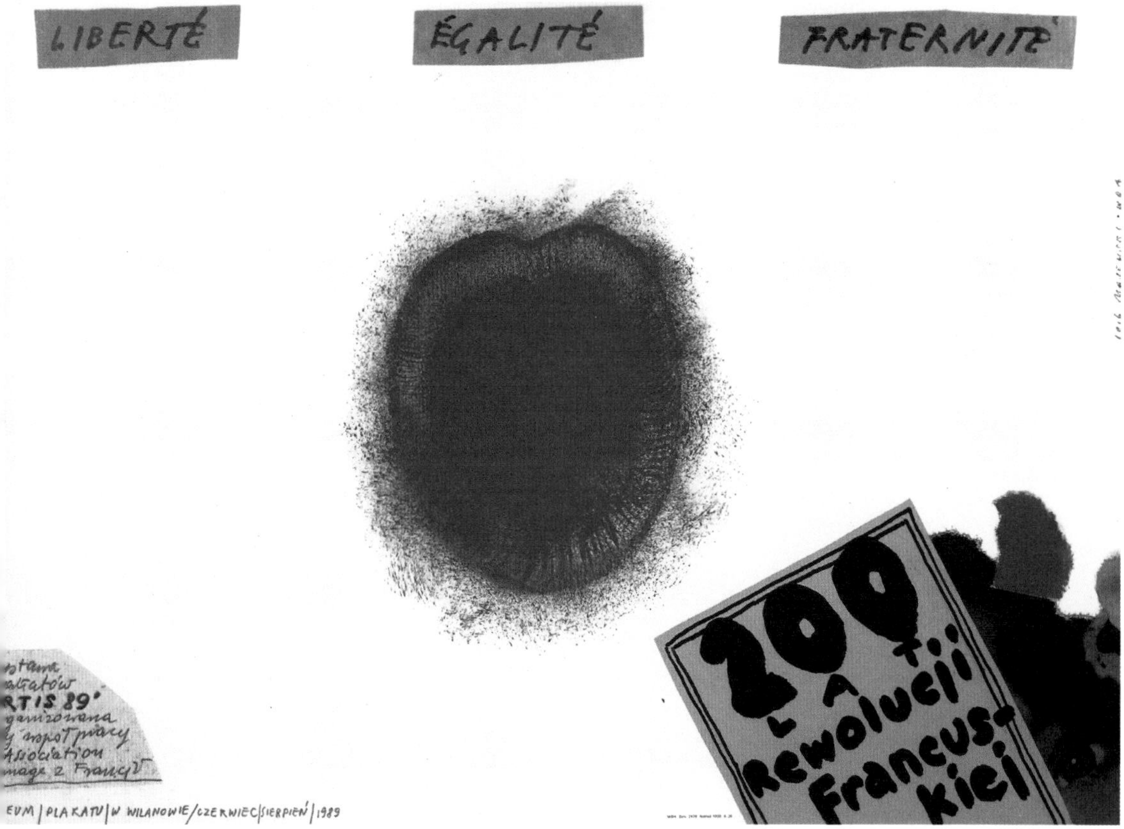
LIBERTÉ
ÉGALITÉ
FRATERNITÉ
200 LAT Rewolucji Francus-kiej
RTIS 89'
EUM | PLAKATU | W WILANOWIE / CZERWIEC | SIERPIEŃ | 1989

Left: « Holidays for dog ». Film poster. 1981. 68 x 98 cm. Offset. Client: ZRF.
Right above: « Untitled ». Drawing.
Right under: « Balcerzak, painting ». Poster. 1992. 68 x 98 cm. Offset. Client: BWA.

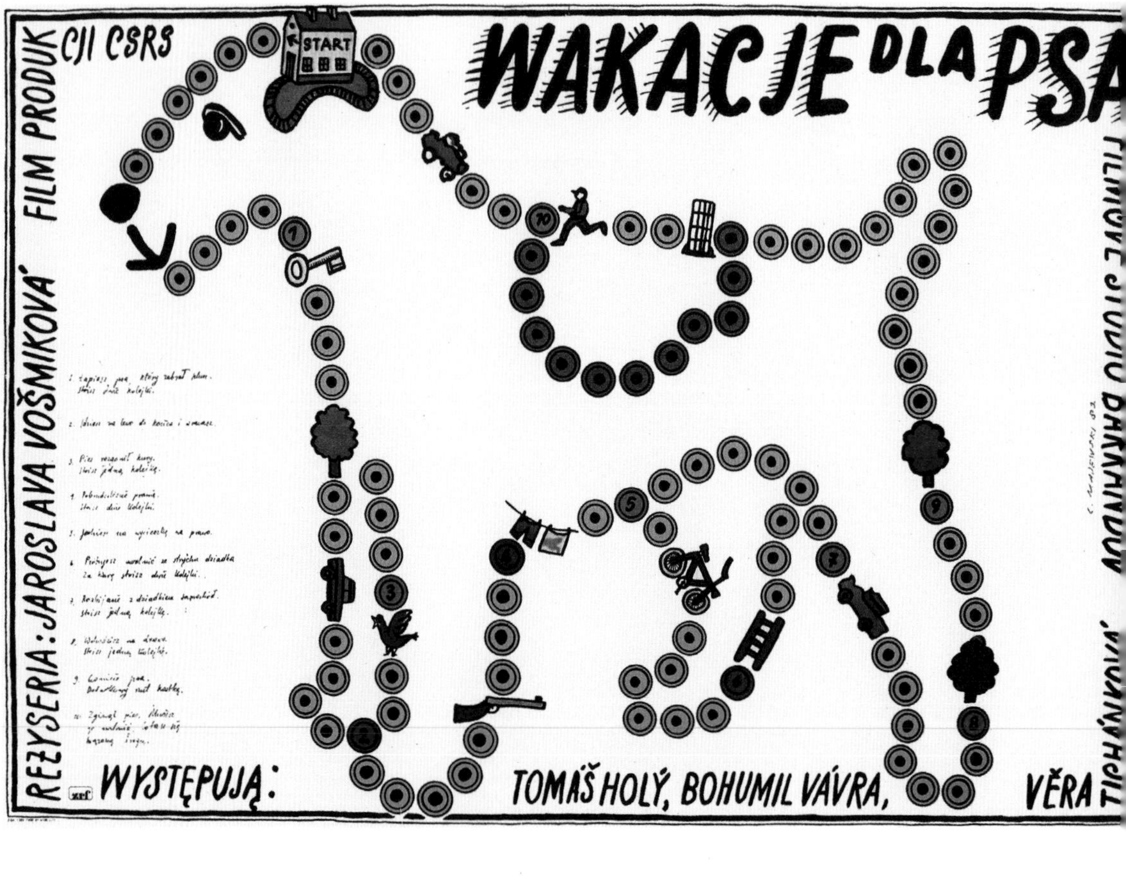

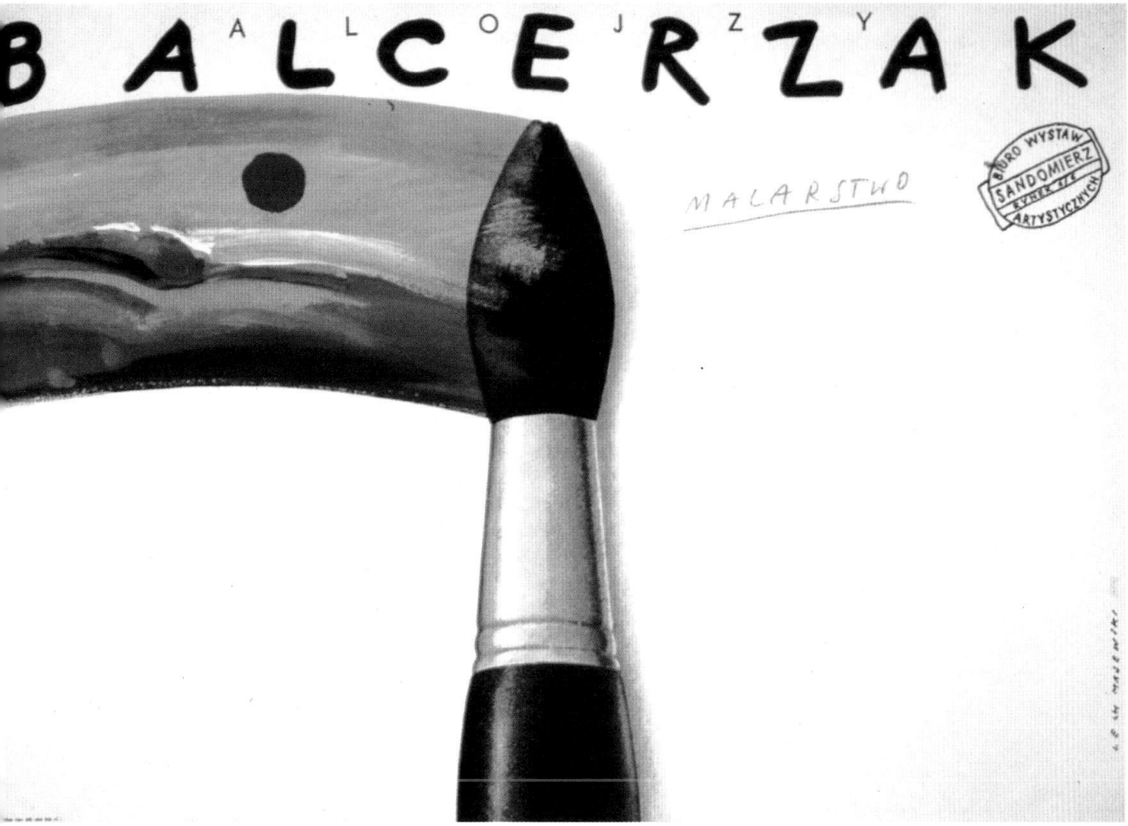
A L O J Z Y
B A L C E R Z A K
MALARSTWO
BIURO WYSTAW ARTYSTYCZNYCH
SANDOMIERZ

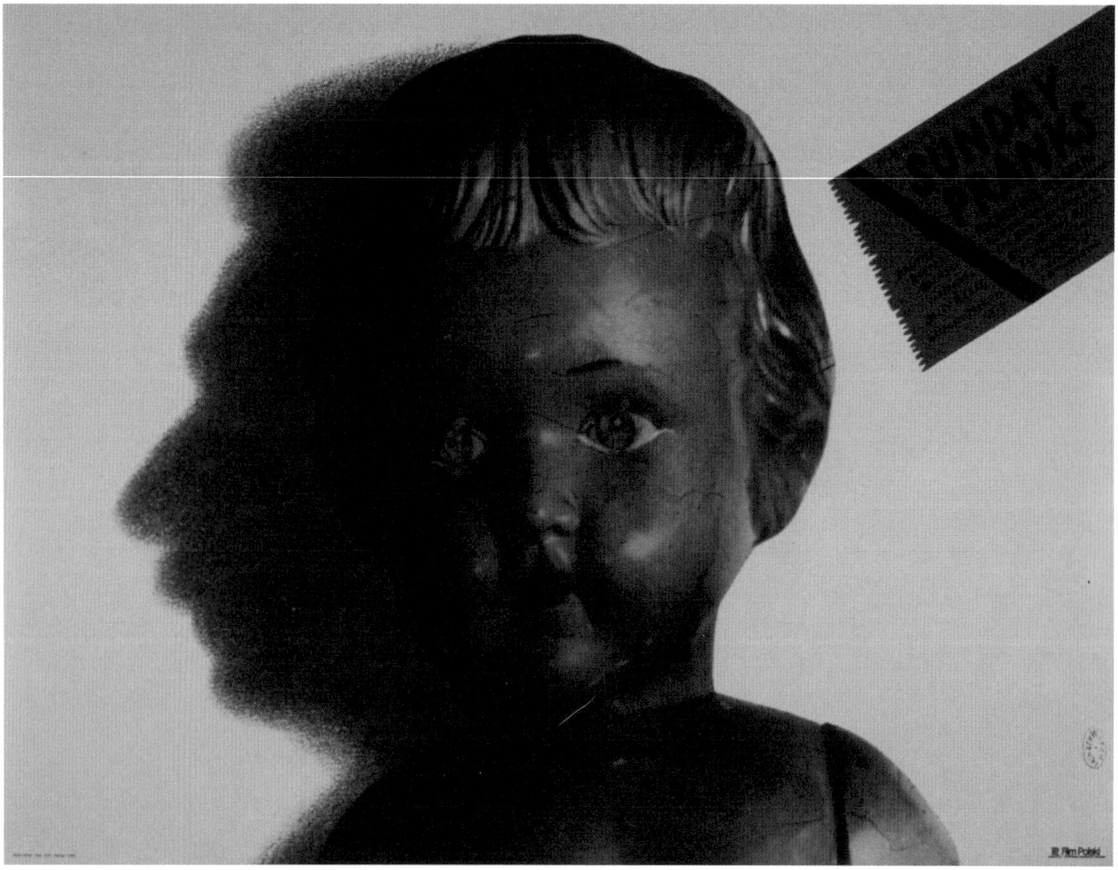

Left above: « Sunday Pranks ». Film poster. 1983. 68 x 98 cm. Offset. Client: Polfilm.
Left under: « Untitled ». Drawing.
Right: « Ball at the Koluszl Station ». Film poster. 1982. 68 x 98 cm. Offset. Client: Polfilm.

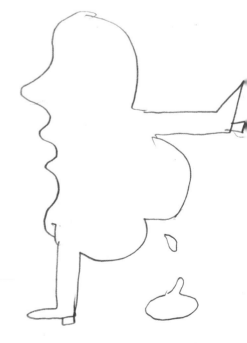

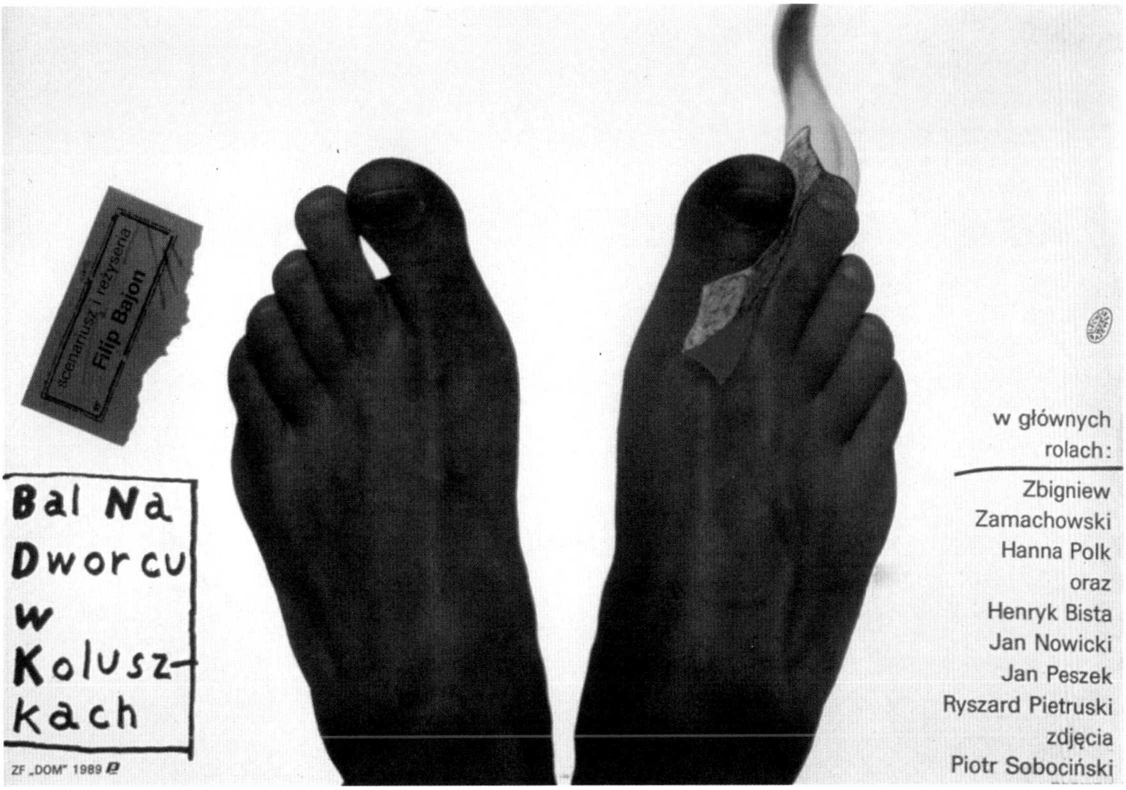
scenariusz i reżyseria
Filip Bajon
Bal Na
Dworcu
w
Kolusz-
kach
ZF „DOM" 1989
w głównych
rolach:
Zbigniew
Zamachowski
Hanna Polk
oraz
Henryk Bista
Jan Nowicki
Jan Peszek
Ryszard Pietruski
zdjęcia
Piotr Sobociński

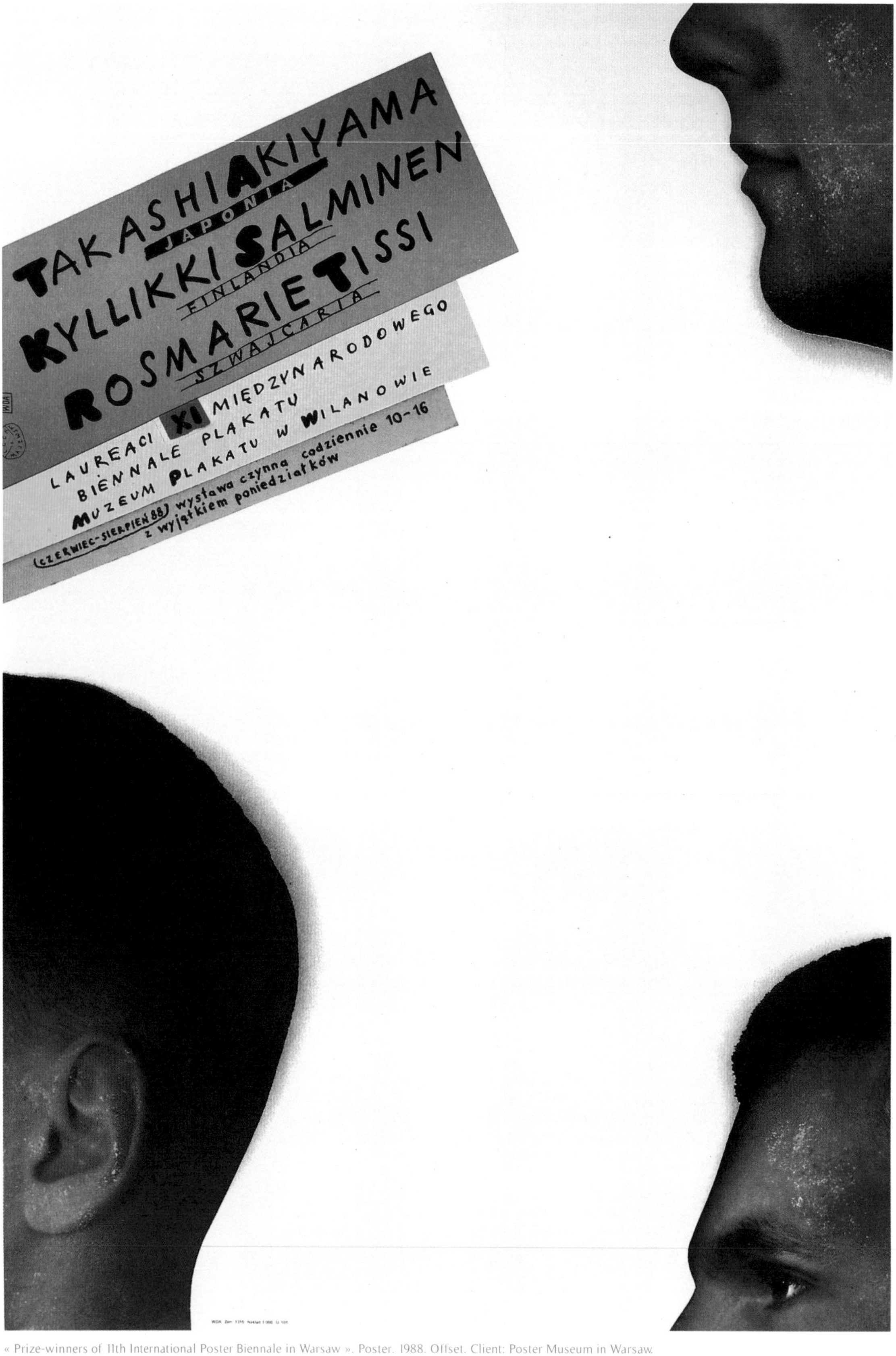

« Prize-winners of 11th International Poster Biennale in Warsaw ». Poster. 1988. Offset. Client: Poster Museum in Warsaw.

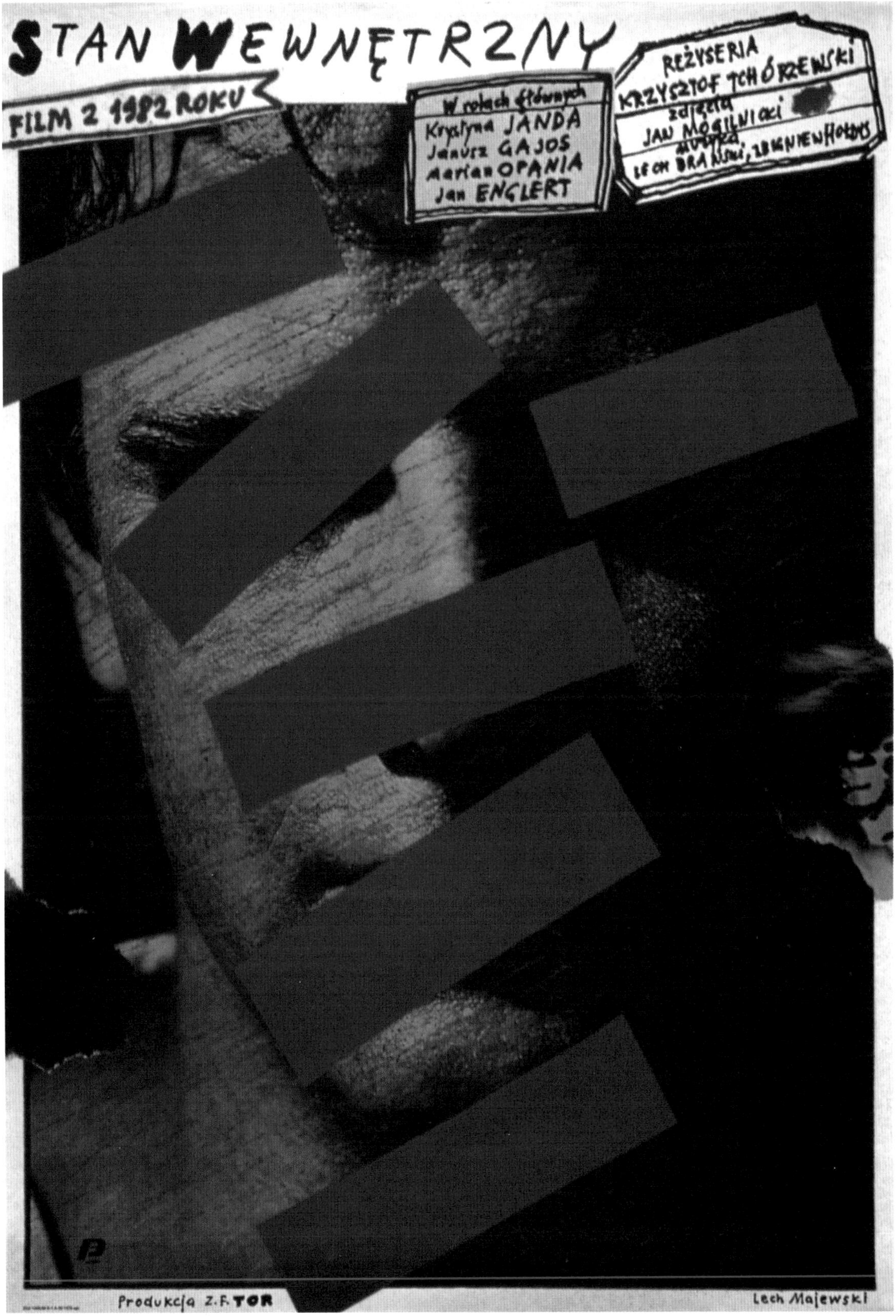

« Inner State ». Film poster. 1983. 98 x 68 cm. Offset. Client: Polfilm.

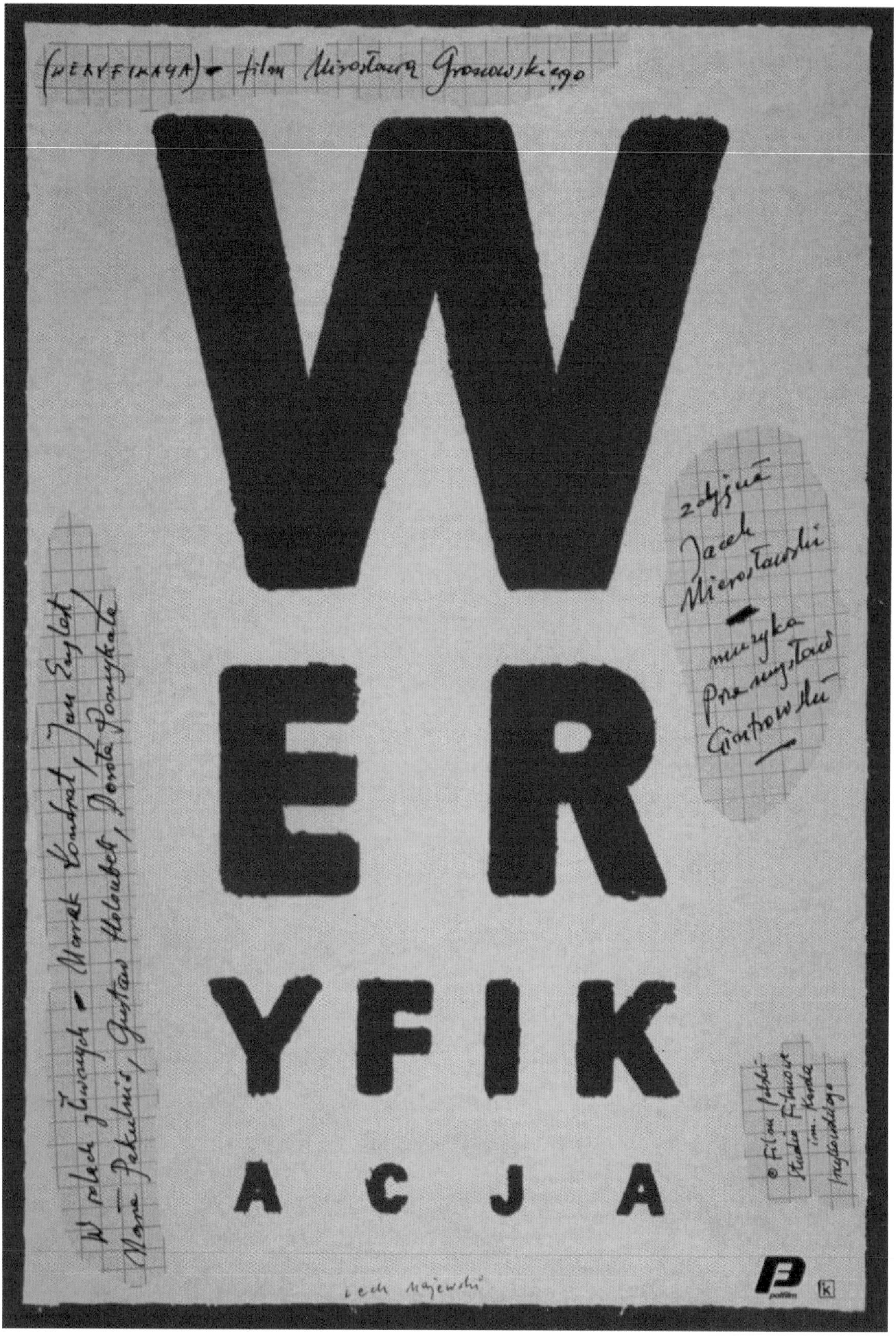

« Verification ». Film poster. 1983. 98 x 68 cm. Offset. Client: Polfilm.

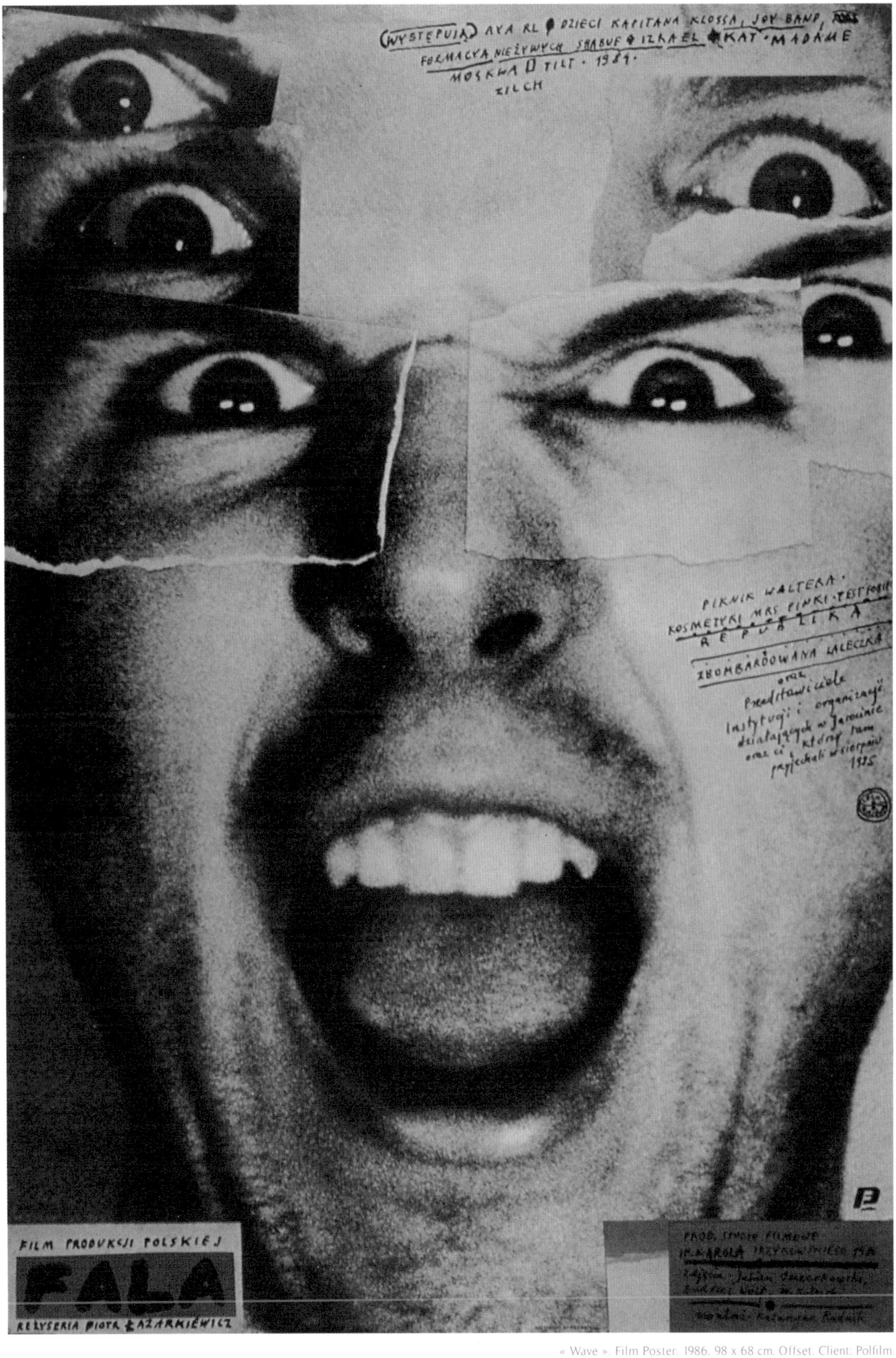

« Wave ». Film Poster. 1986. 98 x 68 cm. Offset. Client: Polfilm.

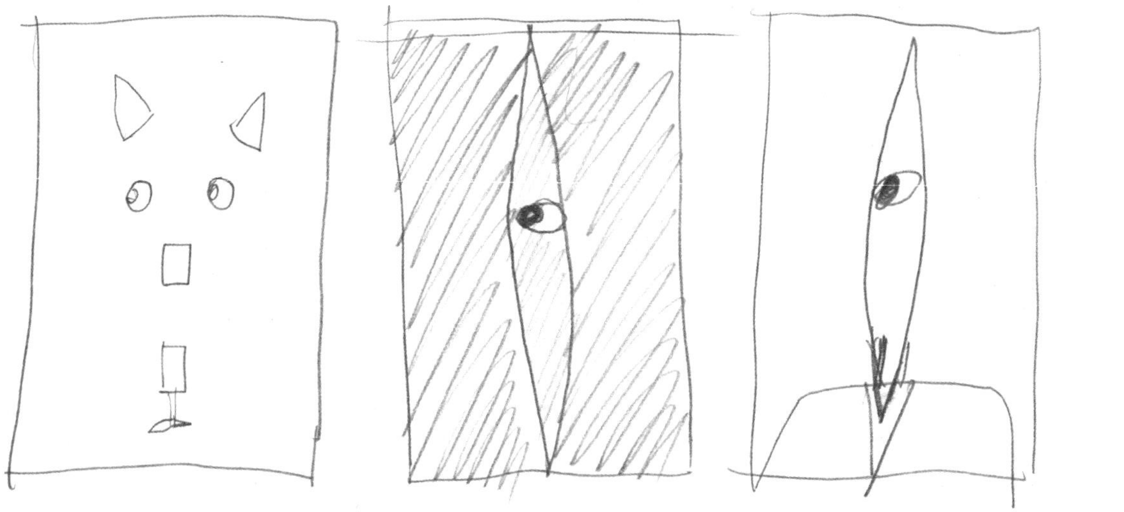

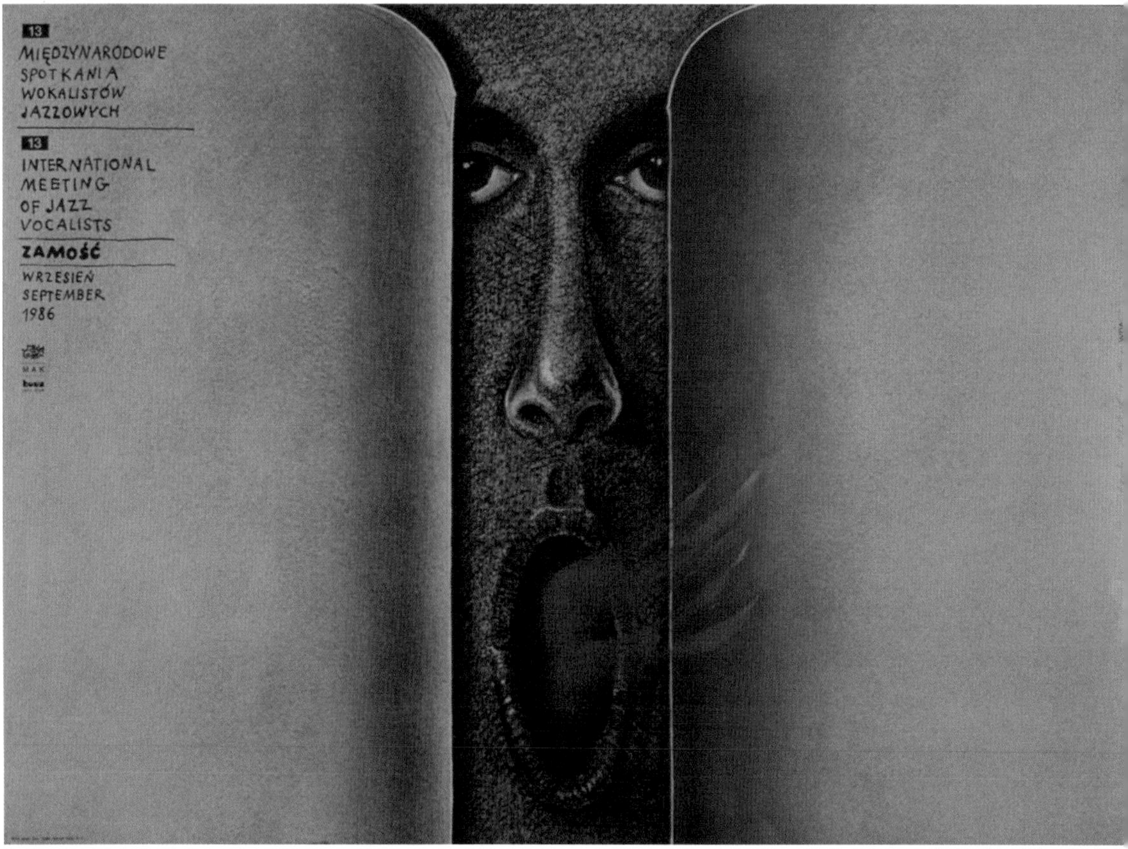
13
MIĘDZYNARODOWE
SPOTKANIA
WOKALISTÓW
JAZZOWYCH
13
INTERNATIONAL
MEETING
OF JAZZ
VOCALISTS
ZAMOŚĆ
WRZESIEŃ
SEPTEMBER
1986
MAK

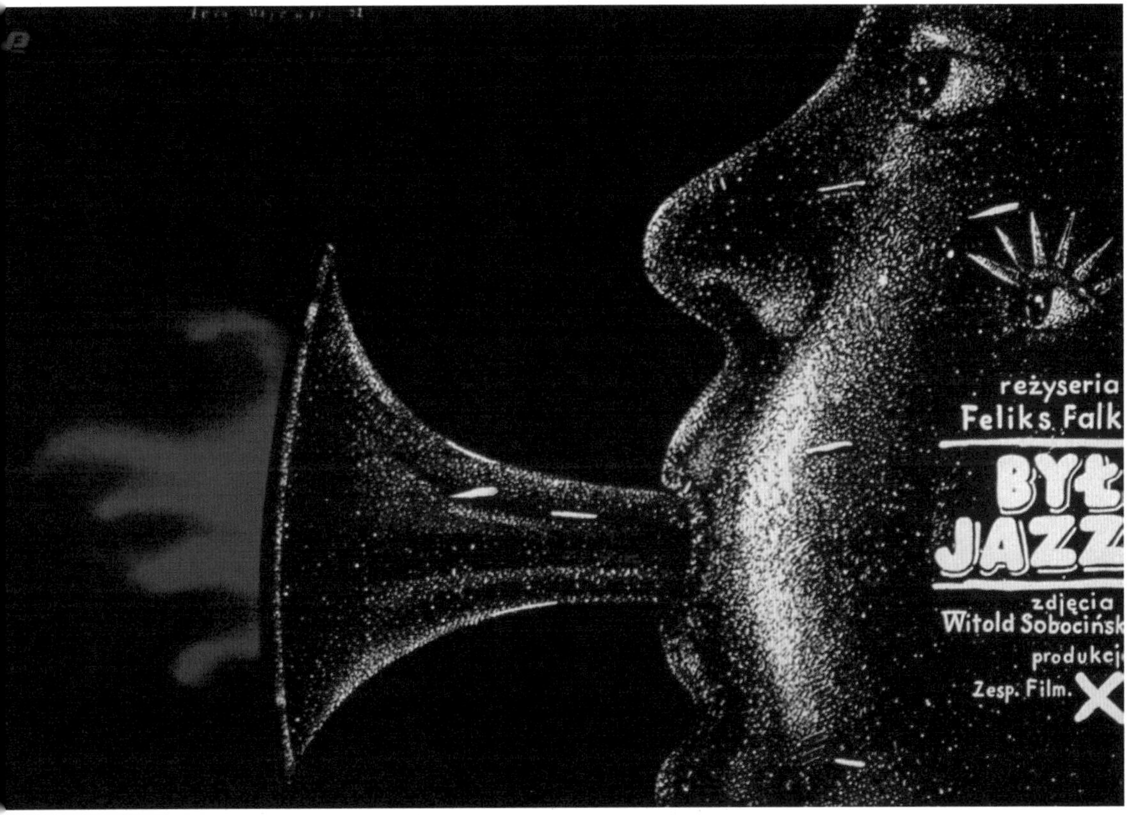

Left above: Sketches for posters. Left under: « Once upon a time there was jazz ». Poster. 68 x 98 cm. Offset. Client: CWF
Right: « Jazz Vocal ». Poster. 1986. 68 x 98 cm. Offset. Client: PSJ. Meeting of jazz vocalists in Zamosc.

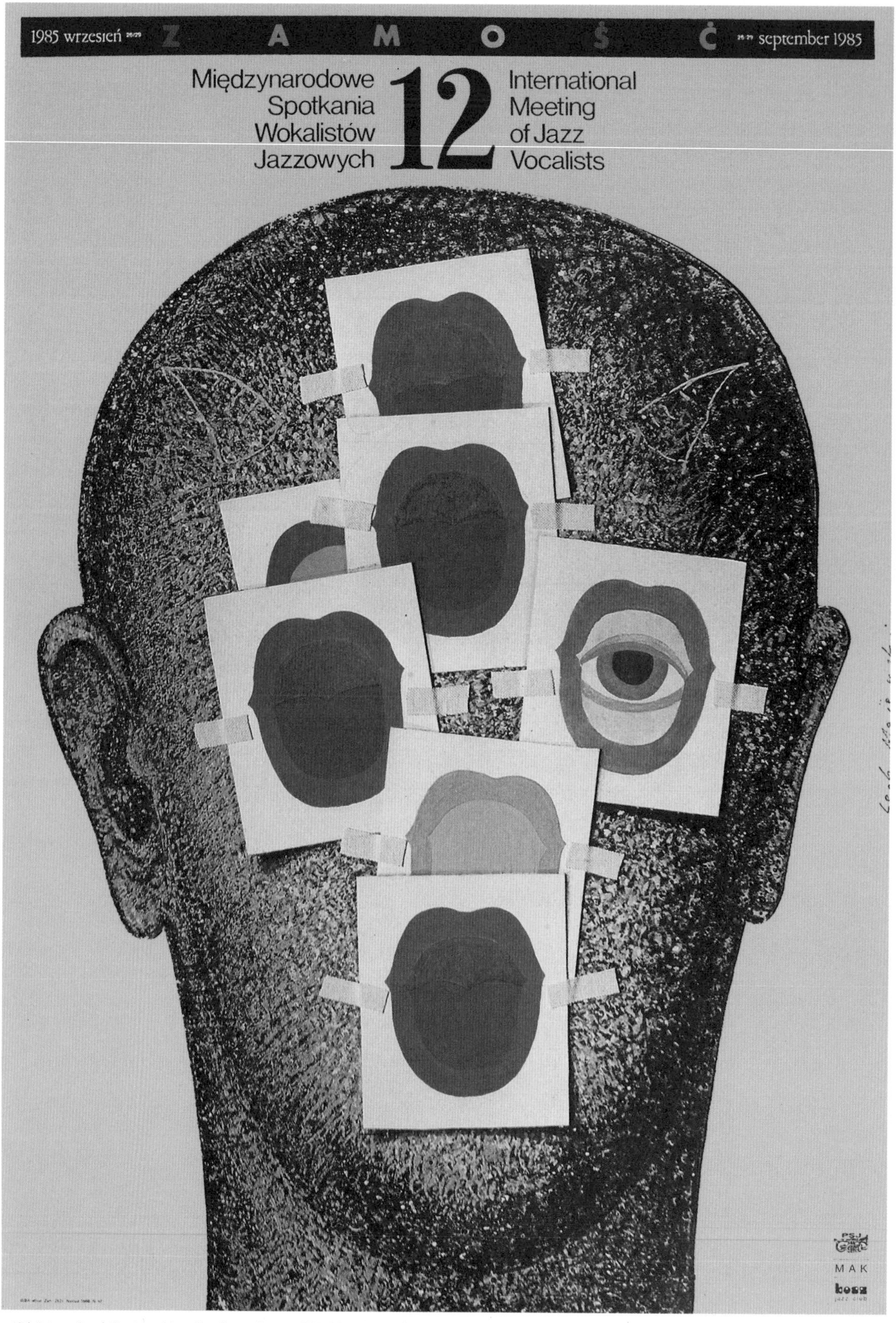

« 12th International Meeting of Jazz Vocalists ». Poster. 1985. 98 x 68 cm. Silk screen. Client: PSJ.

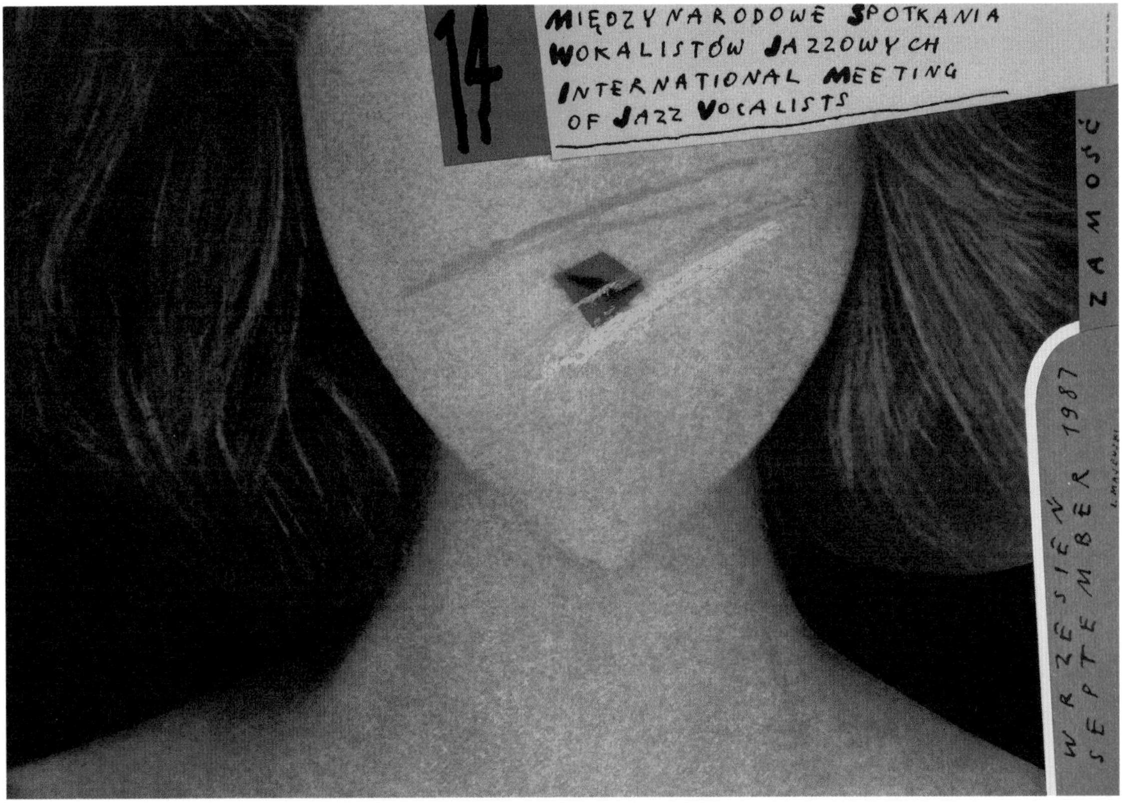

« 14th International Meeting of Jazz Vocalists ». Poster. 1987. 68 x 98 cm. Offset. Client: PSJ. Meeting of jazz vocalists in Zamosc.

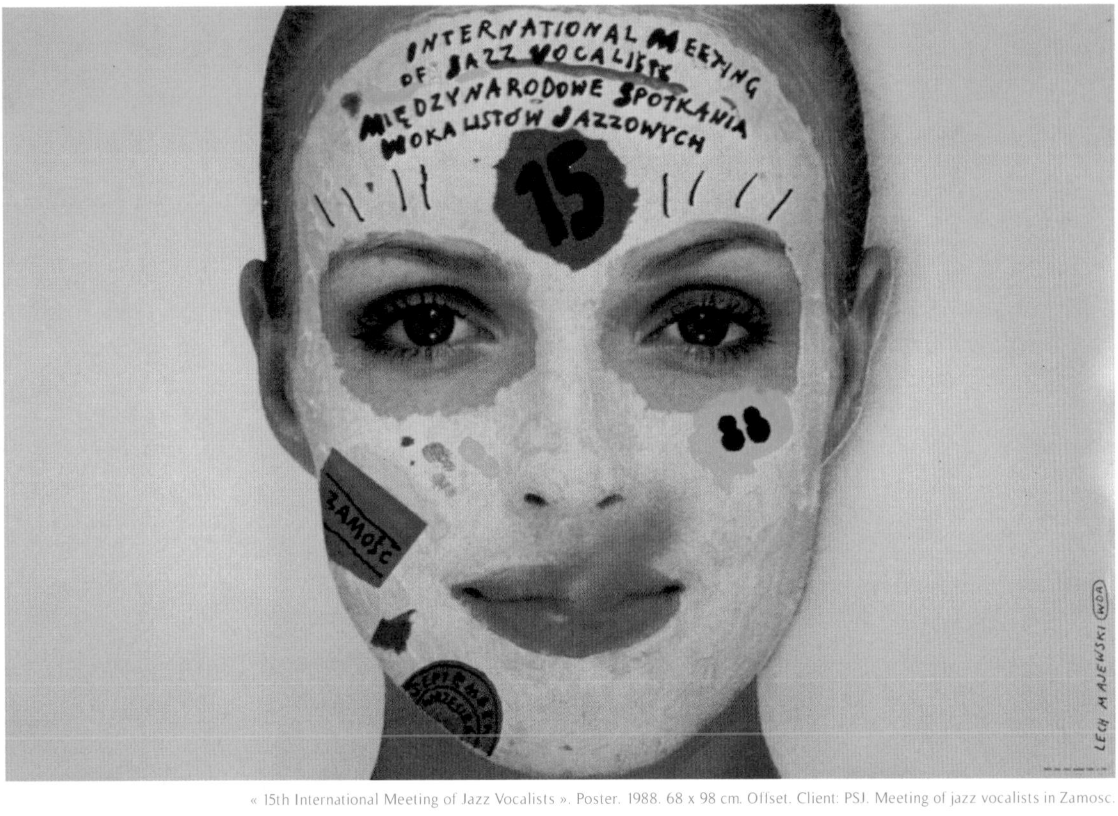

« 15th International Meeting of Jazz Vocalists ». Poster. 1988. 68 x 98 cm. Offset. Client: PSJ. Meeting of jazz vocalists in Zamosc.

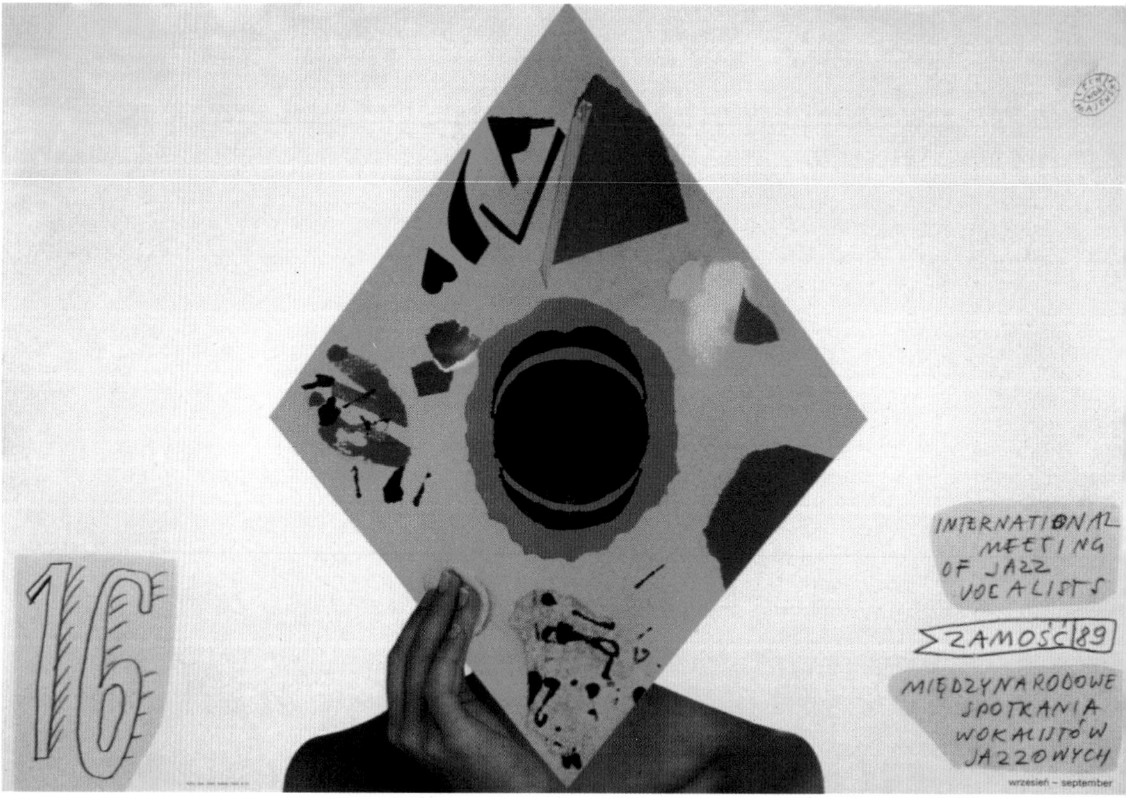
16
INTERNATIONAL MEETING OF JAZZ VOCALISTS
ZAMOŚĆ 89
MIĘDZYNARODOWE SPOTKANIA WOKALISTÓW JAZZOWYCH
wrzesień – september

INTERNATIONAL MEETING OF JAZZ VOCALISTS
ZAMOŚĆ 90
MIĘDZYNARODOWE SPOTKANIA WOKALISTÓW JAZZOWYCH
wrzesień – september
17

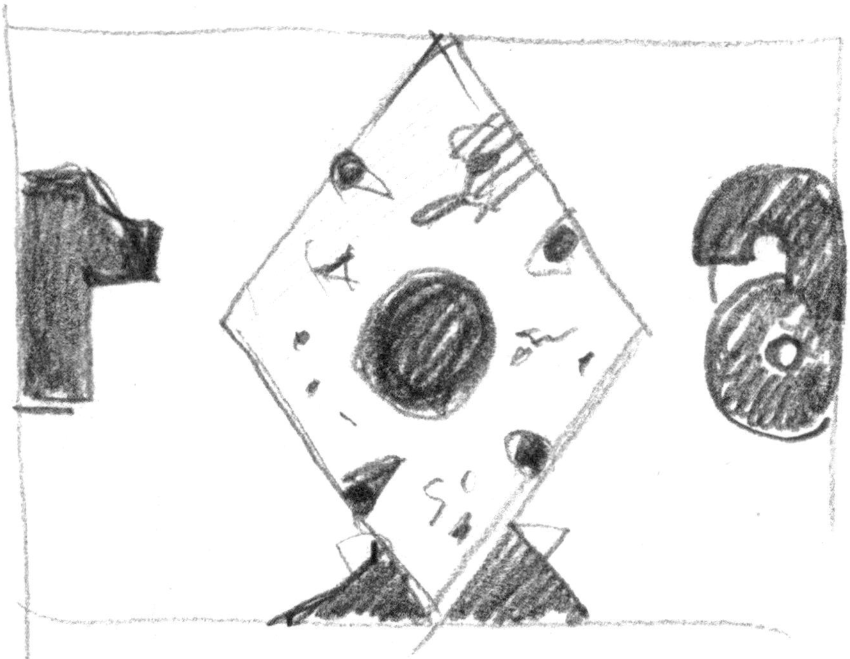

« 16th International Meeting of Jazz Vocalists ». Sketches for the poster. 1989.
« 16th International Meeting of Jazz Vocalists ». Poster. 1989. 68 x 98 cm. Offset. Client: PSJ. Meeting of jazz vocalists in Zamosc.
« 17th International Meeting of Jazz Vocalists ». Poster. 1990. 68 x 98 cm. Offset. Client: PSJ. Meeting of jazz vocalists in Zamosc.

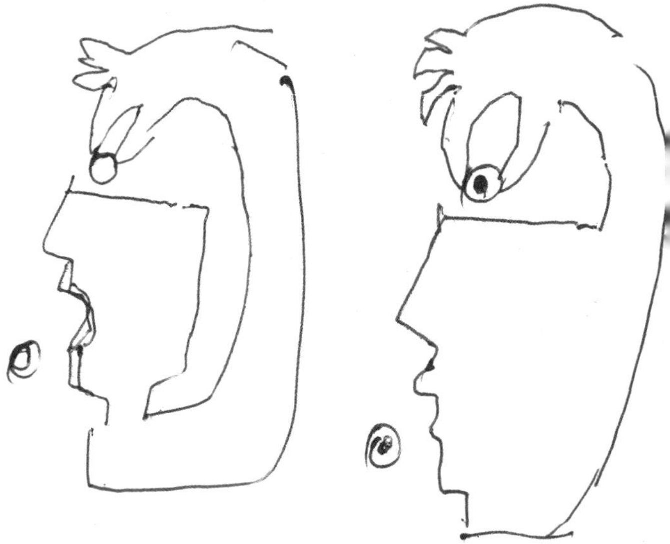

« 19th International Meeting of Jazz Vocalists ». Sketches for the poster. 1992.
« 19th International Meeting of Jazz Vocalists ». Poster. 1992. 68 x 98 cm. Offset. Client: PSJ. Meeting of jazz vocalists in Zamosc.
« 21th International Meeting of Jazz Vocalists ». Poster. 1994. 68 x 98 cm. Silk screen. Client: PSJ. Meeting of jazz vocalists in Zamosc.

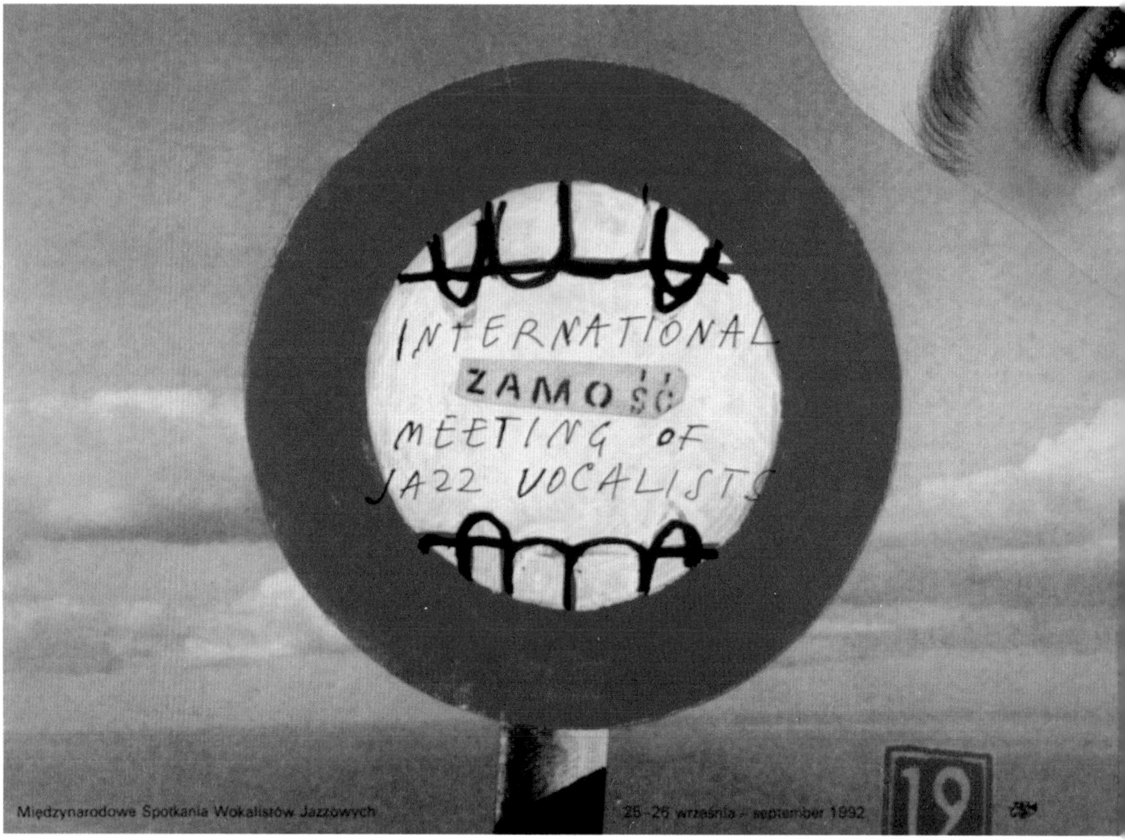

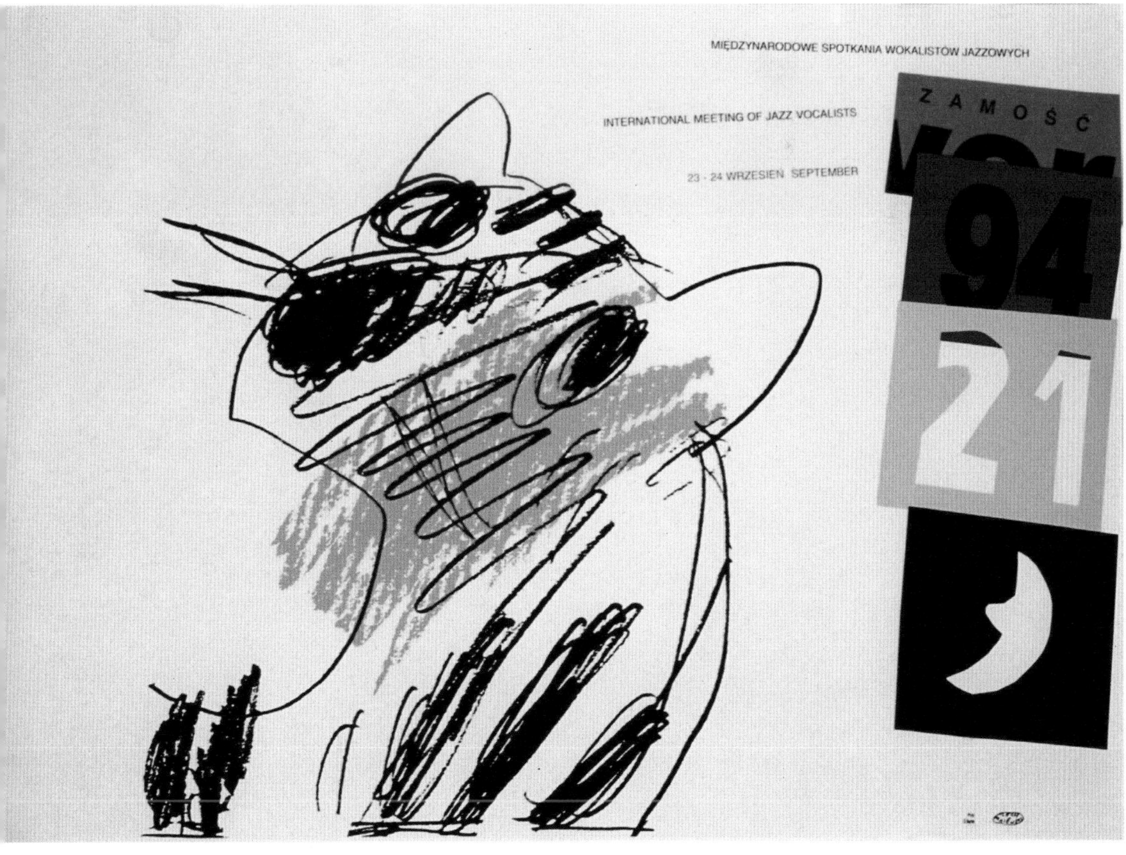
MIĘDZYNARODOWE SPOTKANIA WOKALISTÓW JAZZOWYCH
INTERNATIONAL MEETING OF JAZZ VOCALISTS
23 - 24 WRZESIEN SEPTEMBER
ZAMOŚĆ
94
21

23
International Meeting
of Jazz Vocalists
Międzynarodowe Spotkania
Wokalistów Jazzowych
Zamość 27/28.09.1996
LECH MAJEWSKI

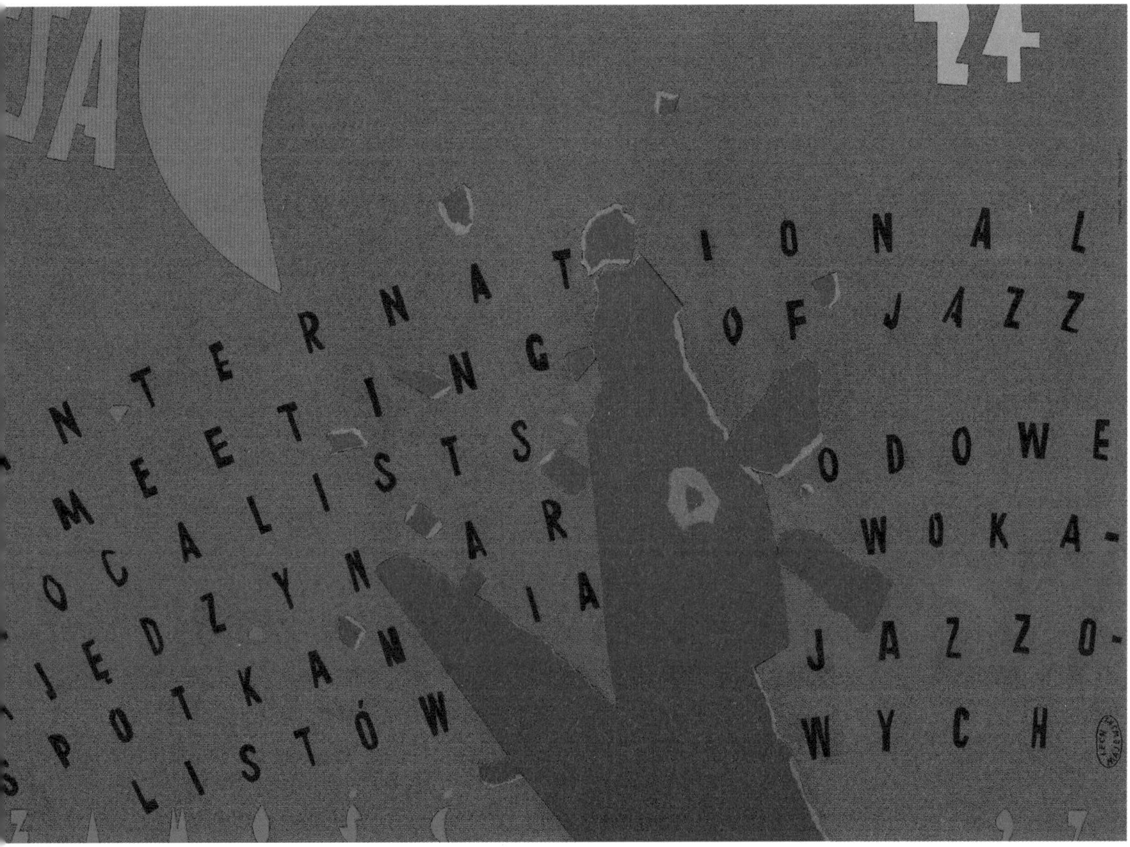

« 23th International Meeting of Jazz Vocalists ». Poster. 1996. 98 x 68 cm. Silk screen. Client: PSJ. Meeting of Jazz Vocalists in Zamosc.
« 24th International Meeting of Jazz Vocalists ». Poster. 1997. 68 x 98 cm. Offset. Client: PSJ. Meeting of jazz vocalists in Zamosc.

« 25th International Meeting of Jazz Vocalists ». Sketches for the poster. 1998.
« 25th International Meeting of Jazz Vocalists ». Poster. 1998. 68 x 98 cm. Offset. Client: PSJ. Meeting of jazz vocalists in Zamosc.

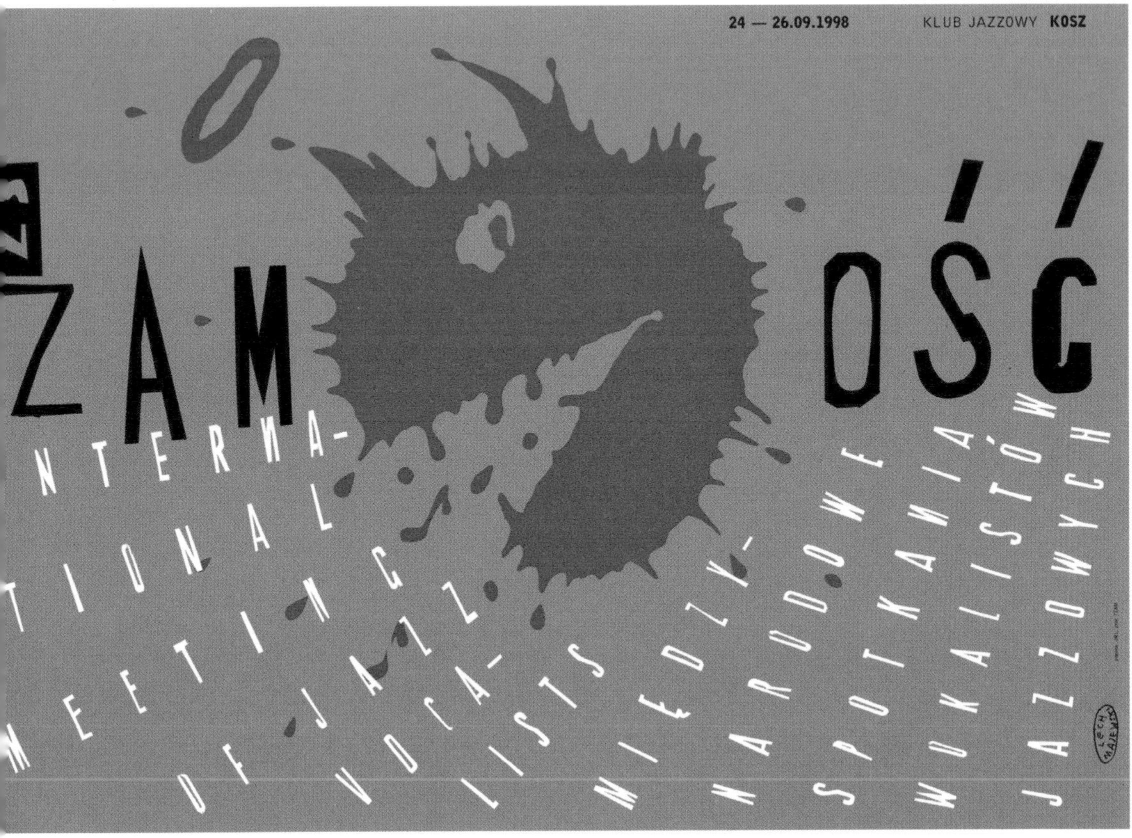
24 — 26.09.1998
KLUB JAZZOWY KOSZ
ZAM OŚĆ
NTERNA-
TIONAL
MEETING
OF JAZZ
VOCA-
LISTS
MIĘDZY-
NARODOWE
SPOTKANIA
WOKALISTÓW
JAZZOWYCH
LECH MAJEWSKI

« Jazz for Ikea ». Poster. 1989. 98 x 68 cm. Offset. Client: Ikea.

Lech Majewski by Michal Warda

Lech Majewski (born in 1947) specializes in editorial and advertising graphics, poster art, graphics in general, and drawing. Since 1996 he has run his own graphic atelier. He graduated from the Faculty of Graphic Arts at the Academy of Fine Arts in Warsaw in 1972, receiving his diploma from Professor Henryk Tomaszewski's Atelier of Posters. He is a professor at the Warsaw Academy of Fine Arts, Dean of the Faculty of Graphic Arts, where he conducts courses at the Atelier of Graphic Design. He is also the Chairman of the Organizing Committee of the International Poster Biennale in Warsaw. He participates in numerous competitions and poster exhibitions all around the world. Lech Majewski's works have won many prizes and distinctions, including those of the Polish Poster Biennale in Katowice, International Poster Biennale, International Poster Exhibition in Paris, International Triennale of Theatre Poster in Rzeszów and Polish Poster Festival in Cracow. In 1986, (together with K. Syta) he was awarded the Prime Minister's Prize for artistic work for children and youth for preparing the design of a mathematic textbook.

In the period of 1988-2004, books and albums designed by Lech Majewski were awarded numerous prizes in the Most Beautiful Book of the Year competition, organized by the Polish Book Editors' Association (including "Crucified" ("Ukrzyżowany") with Piotr Kłosek photographs, KAW 1999, Bożena Kowalska's "Fangor", BoSZ 2002, "Picasso" exhibition catalogue, the National Museum of Warsaw 2002, "Almanach of Polish Illustrators", 2003, "Wolfs" ("Wilki") – Grand Prix 2004). The calendar entitled "Prague" with Monika Patyczek's photographs won two first prizes at the 2003 Vidical calendar competition: for the best calendar with multiple illustrations and for the best designed calendar. The "Vienna" calendar with Tomek Tomaszewski's photographs won the first prize at 2004 Vidical.

Lech Majewski lectures at many European (e.g. in Holland, France, Germany, Switzerland, Italy) and American (e.g. in Brazil, Chile, Mexico) art academies.

Fourteen years ago, Lech Majewski's poster announcing the 16th Edition of the Jazz Vocalists' Festival in Zamość was recognized by design art critics and the Japanese editor Toppan Printing as one of the 100 most important posters from Europe and the USA, created in the period of 1945-90. Works shown in the album constitute an absolute canon of graphic design and are a set of the most eminent achievements of poster art in the second half of the 20th century.

In the history of Polish poster art, the 70's were a period of interesting debuts of new genuine styles in graphic design. Works conceived in the beginnings of Lech Majewski's artistic activity belong to the painting poster stream, using close-ups of the human face. All text information, which was usually drafted by hand, was put to the borders of the composition. A precisely shaped image dominated, in which traditional drawing techniques were merged with the color dynamism of distemper and acryl. In the beginnings of the 80's Majewski abandons colors more and more often; his posters become mostly black-and-white graphics in which a predilection dominates for image-sign acquired at Professor Tomaszewski's atelier. In 1986, the first work announcing a series of the Zamość Jazz Festival posters was created. Majewski began to merge former techniques with photographs. Collage becomes an excellent way to achieve a contrarious, slightly ironic representation of jazz vocalist art. From the beginnings of the 90's, Majewski's work evolved towards a new, presently dominating formula, responding to the contemporary urban street aesthetics. He composes graphically restrained images, using flat, synthetic forms of unified, intensive color. Particularly vivid, expressive graphics, in which a distinctive typography plays an equal role in the image, awkward part of a sentence, break the stereotype of sober theatre poster. Apart from the poster art, Majewski finds the most satisfaction in working on albums, where the issue of using the available illustratory material, as well as typographic and composition issues require full engagement in the process of building the concept of the project.

He treats each and every editing work as an object – a closed entity with its own specific rhythm of narration, resembling a film sequence moving in front of the reader's eyes. Majewski plays the role of a director, constructing the graphic layout of the book on the basis of the available text/scenario. The first contact of the reader with the book takes place through vision, which explains the multitude of revolutionary solutions, breaking traditional barriers that we can find in Majewski's projects; sometimes, he tends to shape the layout of the material in cooperation with the author in order to achieve the visual attractiveness of the text. What Polish editors are often unconcious of is that the book cover fulfills an advertising function; this should lead to the usage of a whole range of graphic resources, from a distinctive sign, and vibrant colors, to a legible typography, as it is in the case of the poster art. Majewski successfully employs his poster designer's experience and makes use of the sign – a contrarious, graphic aphorism, which brilliantly announces the content of the book. On the cover of Helmut Bauer's album entitled "Setz Dich!" (München Stadtmuseum 2000), which was devoted to the history of chair, we find a figure sitting in the void of a black background.

« Untitled ». Drawing.

"Polish Illustrators for Children Almanach" (ZPAP 2003) is announced by a striding book cut out from the cardboard of the jacket, through which we can see a part of a fanciful illustration by Józef Wilkoń. On the title card of the album "Photographs of Tatras and Zakopane 1859-1914" (BoSZ, 2000) the vertical inscription "Tatry" is presented in an escaping perspective of a summit rising beyond the horizon. Since nearly the beginning, Lech Majewski has been combining his professional activity with didactic work at the Warsaw Academy of Fine Arts. He transmits to subsequent generations of future graphic designers the rules of intelligent project creation he himself acquired from Professor Tomaszewski's atelier. He willingly repeats one sentence which summarizes best his attitude towards technologies used in utilitarian graphic art and constitutes the motto of his atelier: we conceive projects in our heads, not on the computer. The basis of the process of creating a project is an idea preserved in the form of a draft made by hand. The computer is only a tool for achieving it. This traditional attitude toward cultivating excellent manual skills forms an individual style and avoids the omnipresent anonymity of computer design. Lech Majewski's method consists of looking permanently for surprising associations breaking the author's and receiver's habits. Following this rule although it may involve some risk determines the value of the design art, which the author ironically mentioned announcing his last year's exhibition of posters and books.

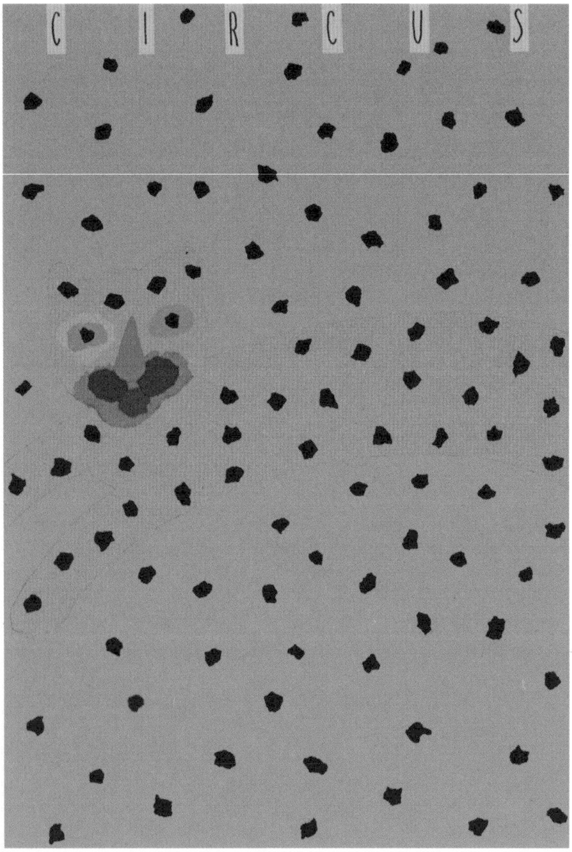

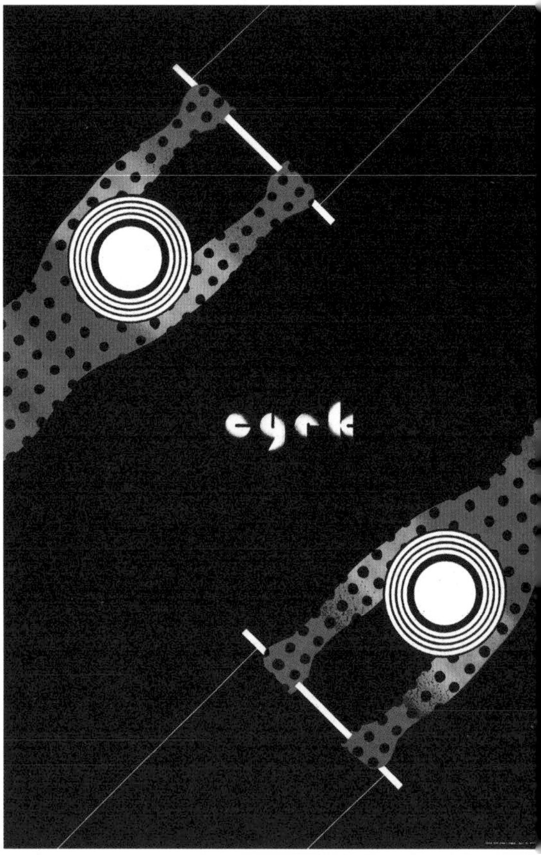

« Circus ». Poster. 1972. 98 x 68 cm. Offset. Client: Ikea.
« Circus ». Poster. 1973. 98 x 68 cm. Offset.

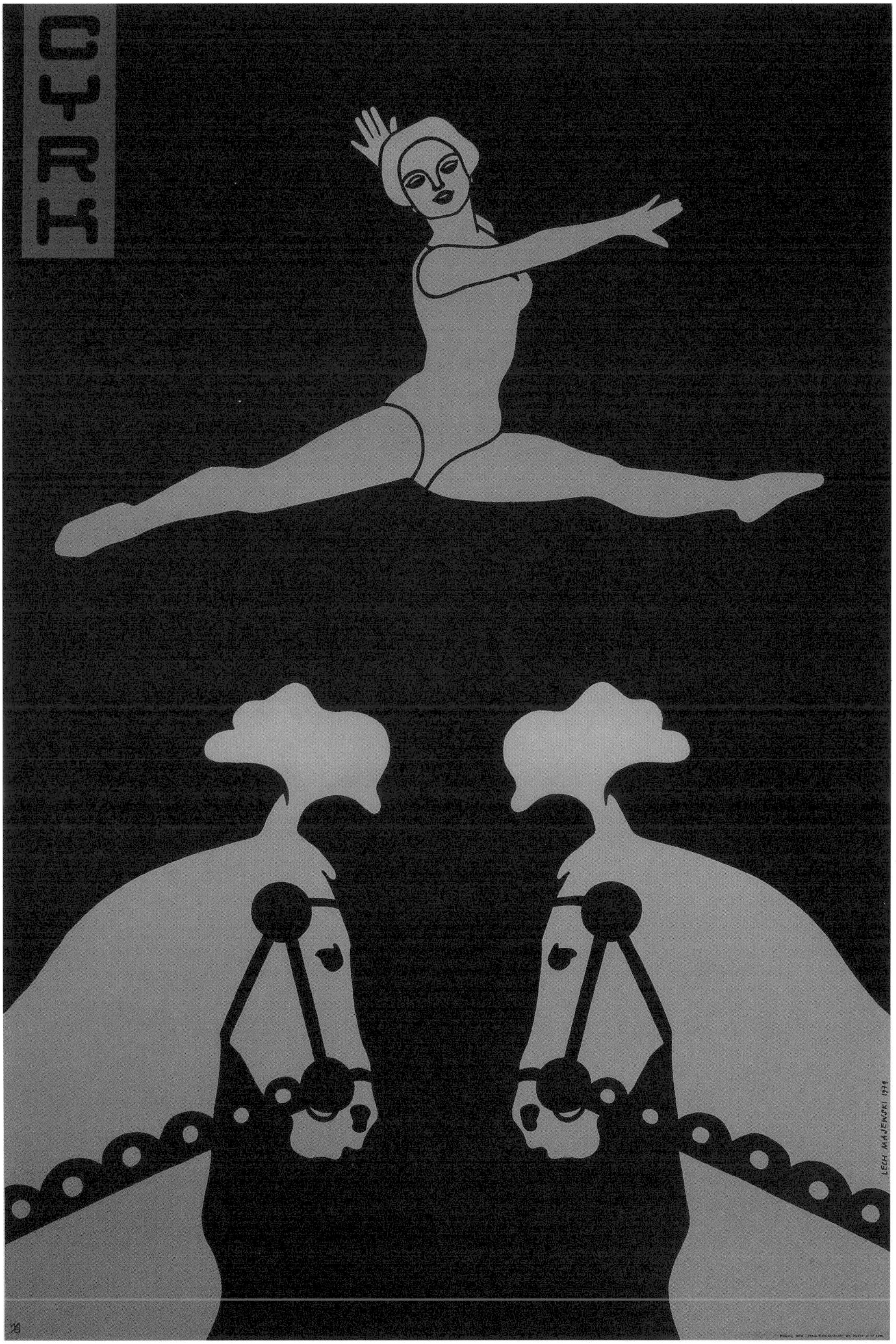

« Circus ». Poster. 1974. 98 x 68 cm. Offset. Client: KAW.

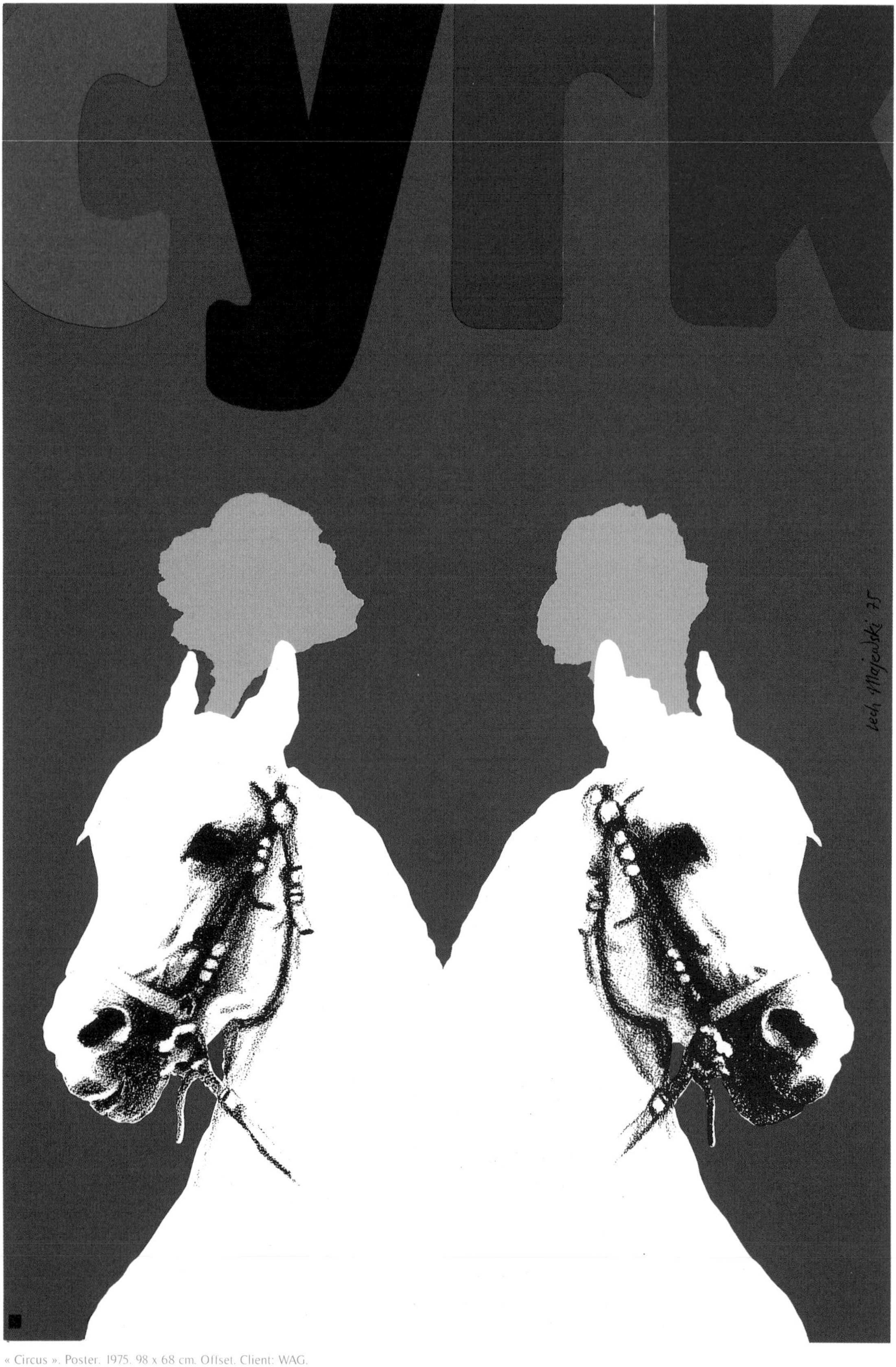

« Circus ». Poster. 1975. 98 x 68 cm. Offset. Client: WAG.

« Untitled ». Drawing.

Above: « Poster Biennale of Theatre ». Poster. 1999. 98 x 68 cm. Offset. Client: Theatre in Rzezow.
Under: « Poster Biennale of Theatre ». Sketches for the poster. 1999.

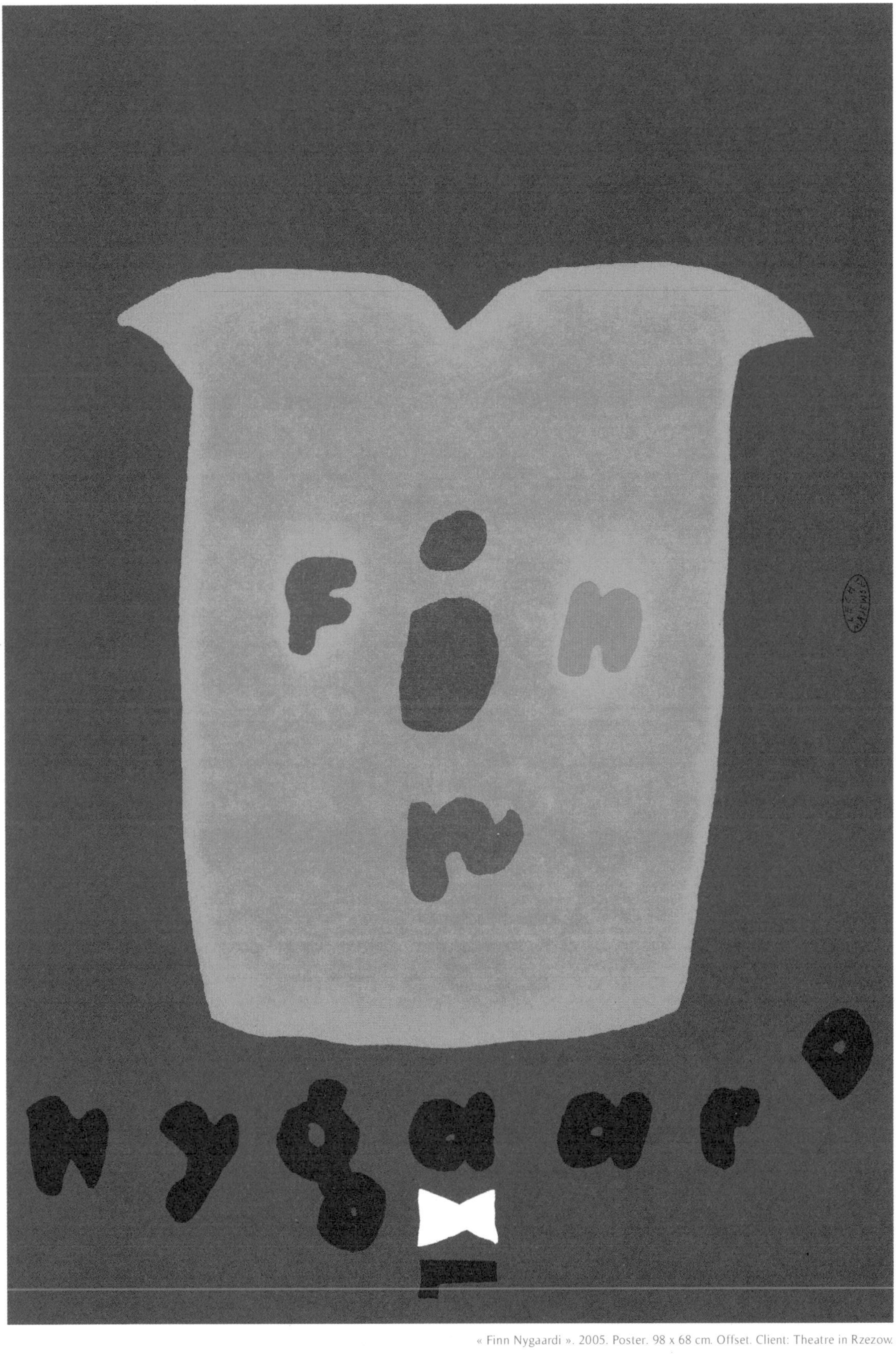

« Finn Nygaardi ». 2005. Poster. 98 x 68 cm. Offset. Client: Theatre in Rzezow.

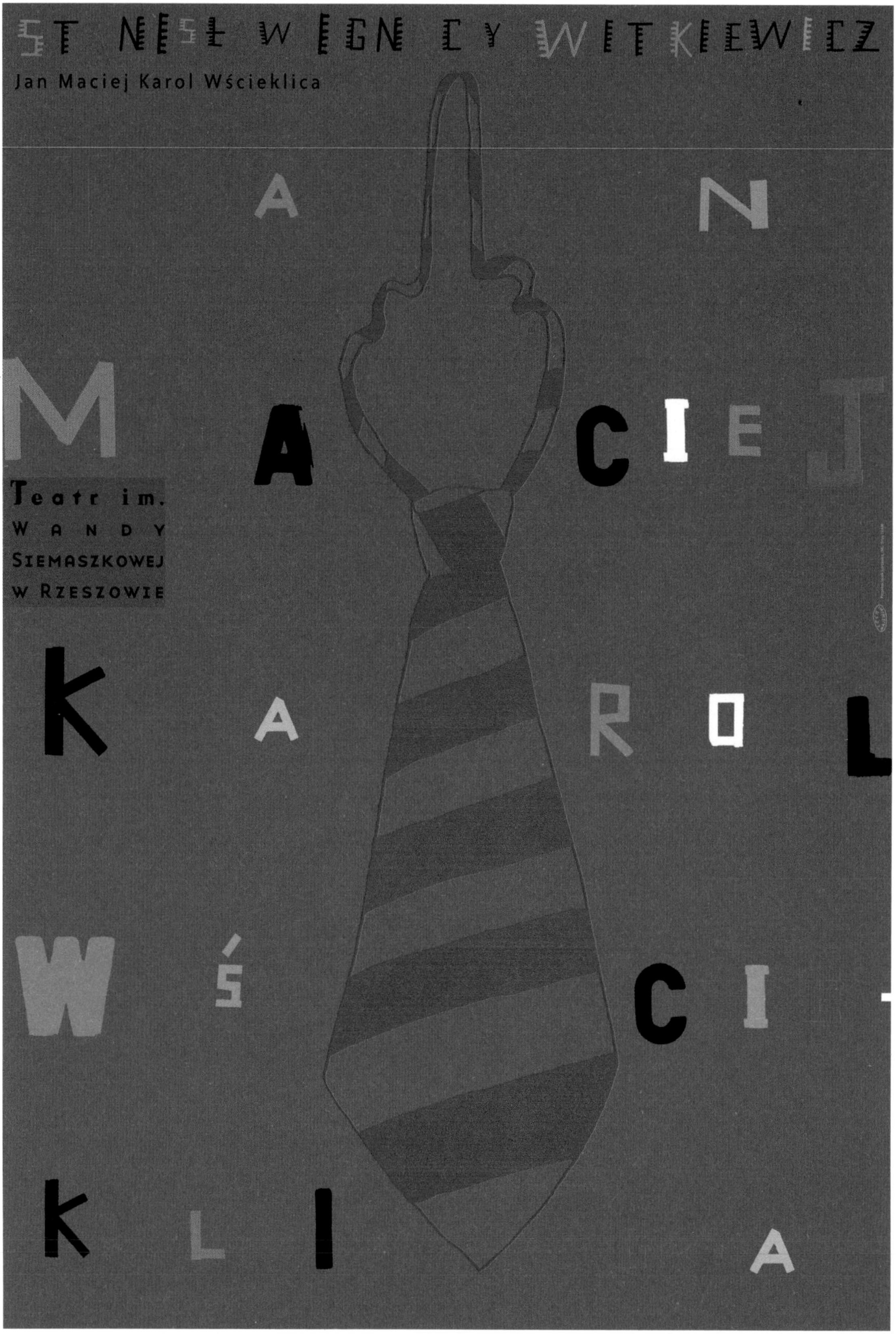

« Wscieklica ». Poster. 2004. 98 x 68 cm. Offset. Client: Rzestow Theatre.

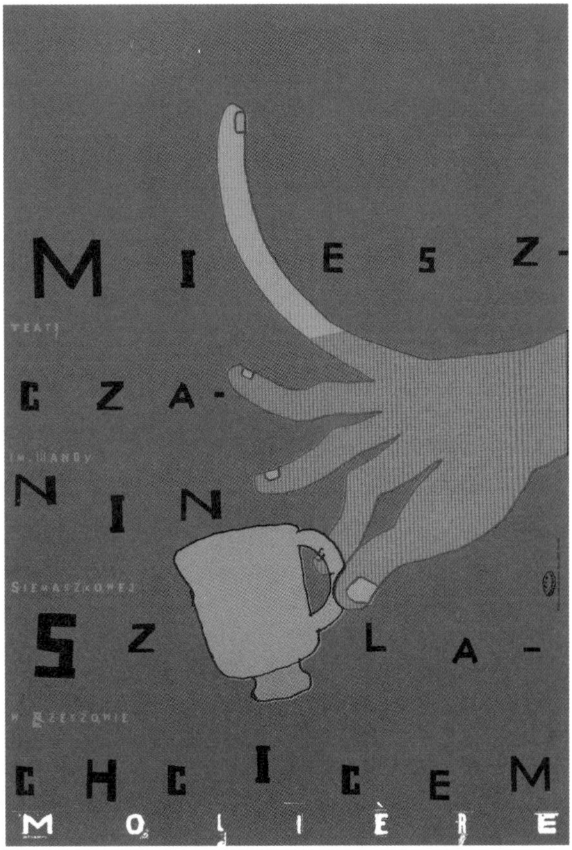

Left: « Wscieklica ». Sketches for the poster. 2004.
Right: « Mieszczanin Salachicem ». Poster. 2004. 98 x 68 cm. Offset. Client: Reszow Theatre.

« Mazepa ». Sketches for the poster. 2003.

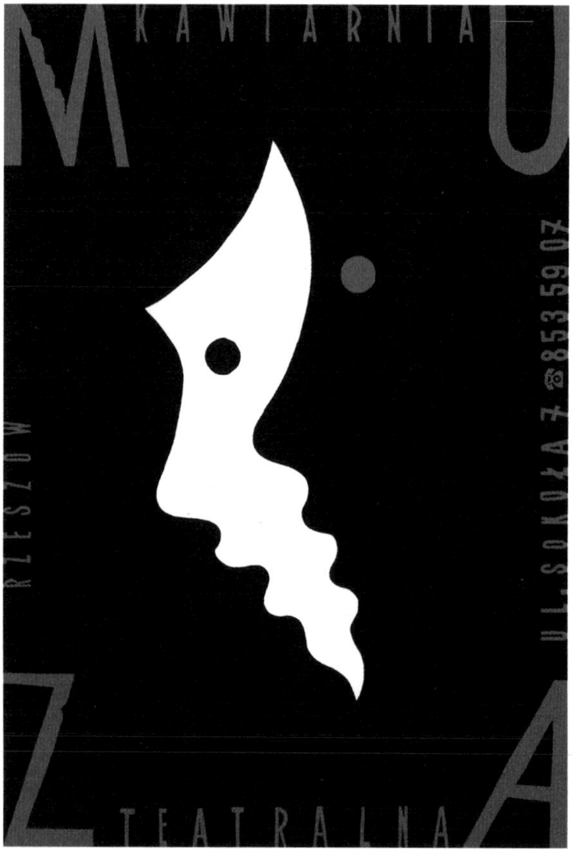

« Cafe Muse ». Poster. 98 x 68 cm. Offset. Client: Reszow Theatre.

« Our God's Brother ». Poster. 98 x 68 cm. Offset. Client: Reszow Theatre.

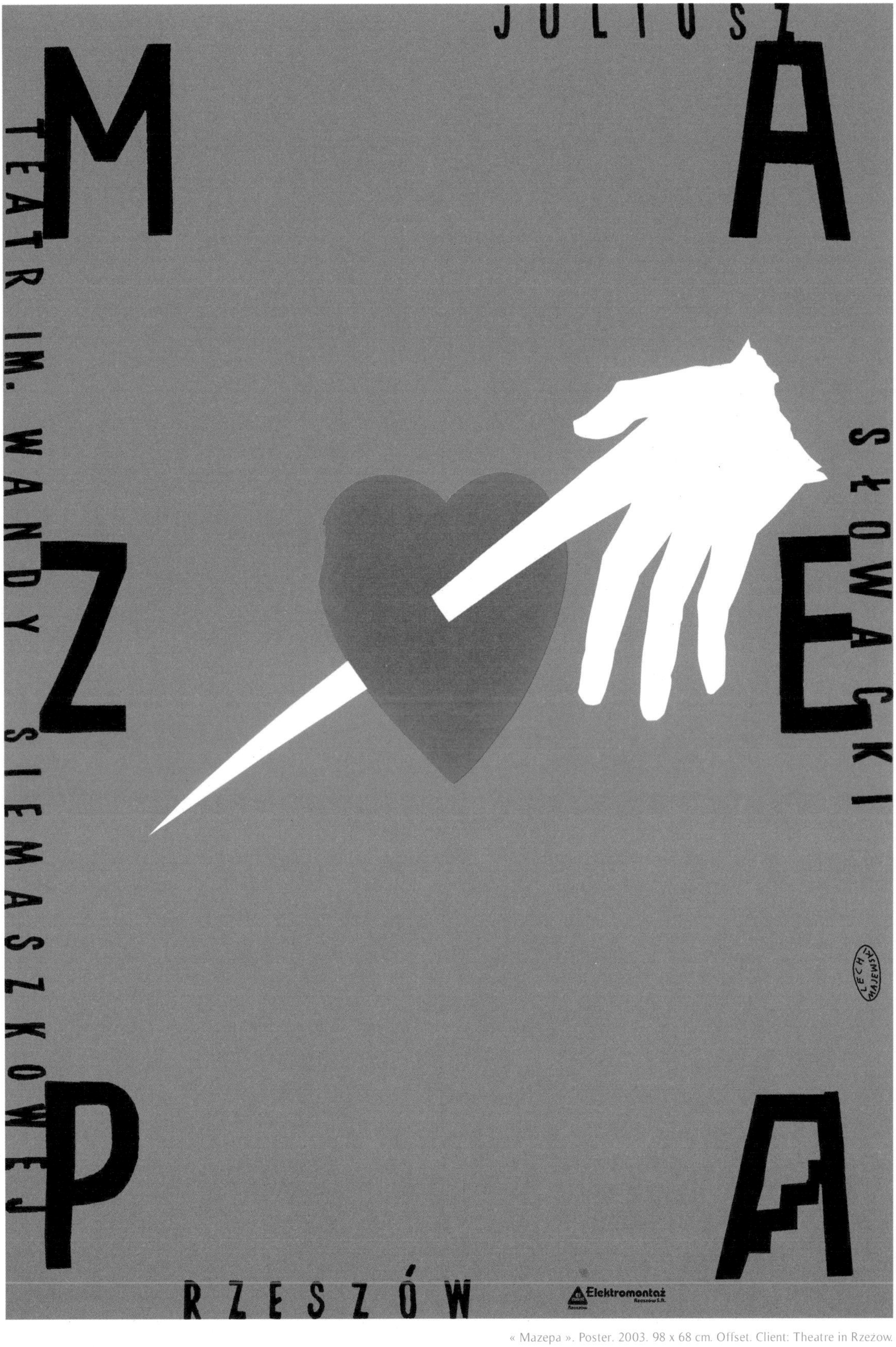

« Mazepa ». Poster. 2003. 98 x 68 cm. Offset. Client: Theatre in Rzeżow.

« Ball at the Opera ». Poster. 1999. 98 x 68 cm. Offset. Client: Reszow Theatre.

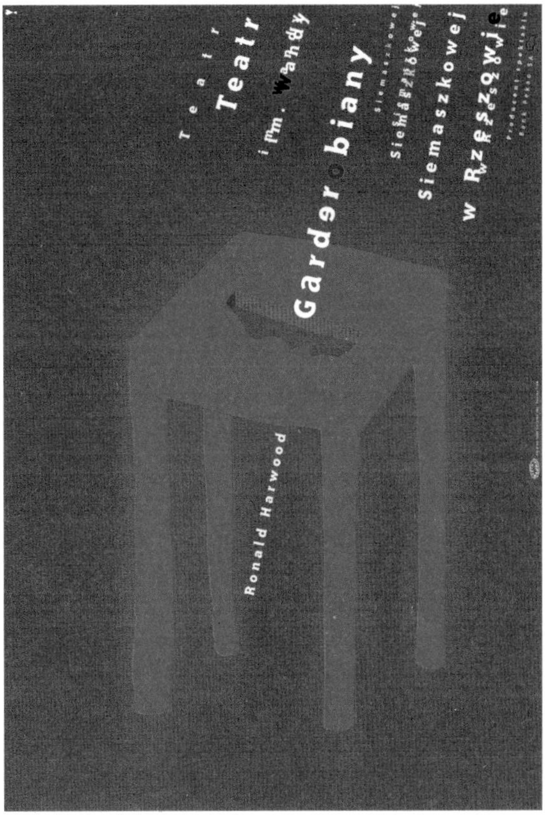

Left: « Ball at the Opera ». Sketches for the poster. 1999.
Above: « Dresser ». Poster. 2003. 98 x 68 cm. Offset. Client: Reszow Theatre.
Under: « Balladyna ». Poster. 2005. 98 x 68 cm. Offset. Client: Theatre in Rzezow.

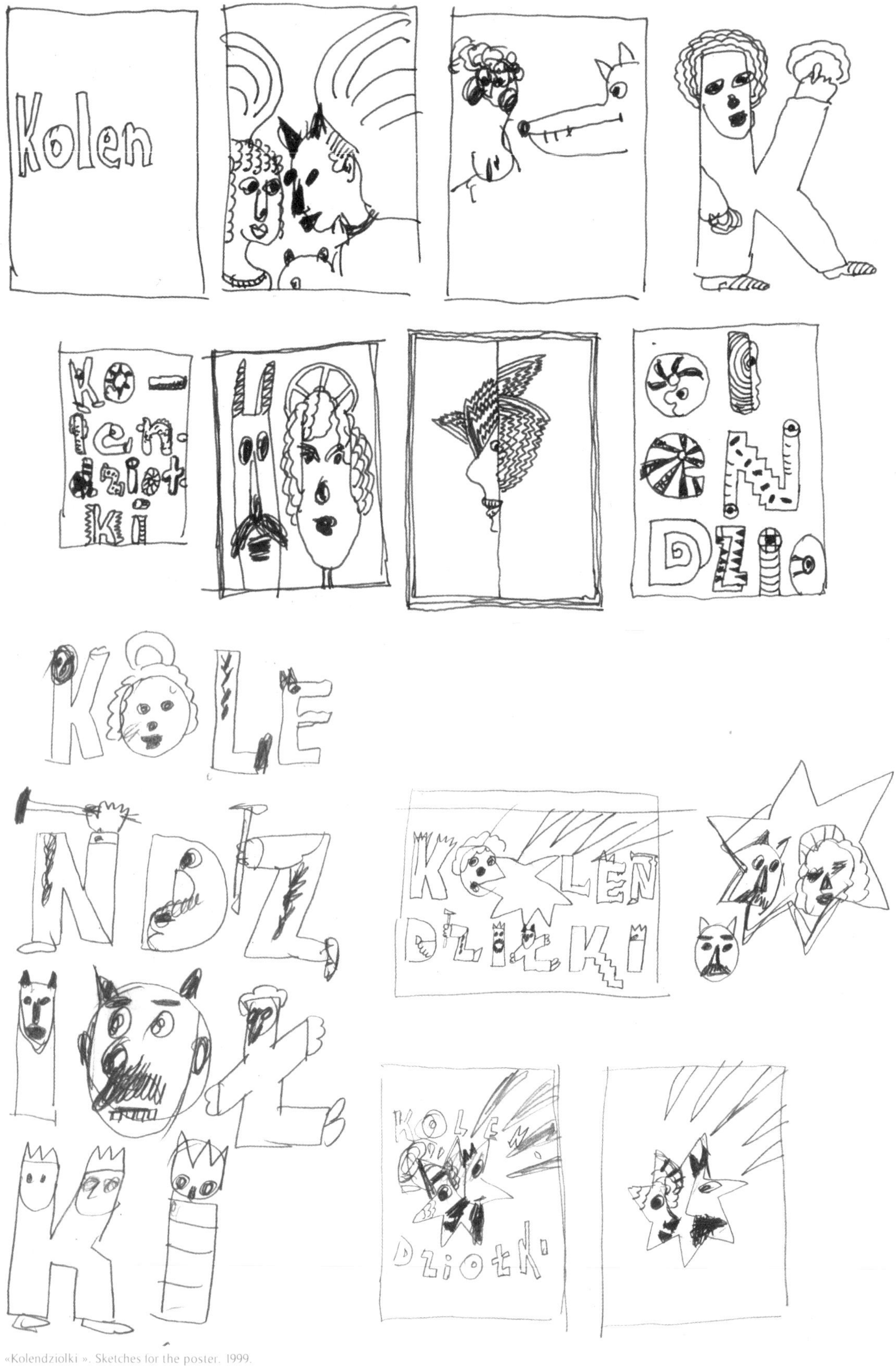

«Kolendziolki». Sketches for the poster. 1999.

«Kolendziolki ». Poster. 1999. 98 x 68 cm. Offset. Client: Theatre in Rzezow.

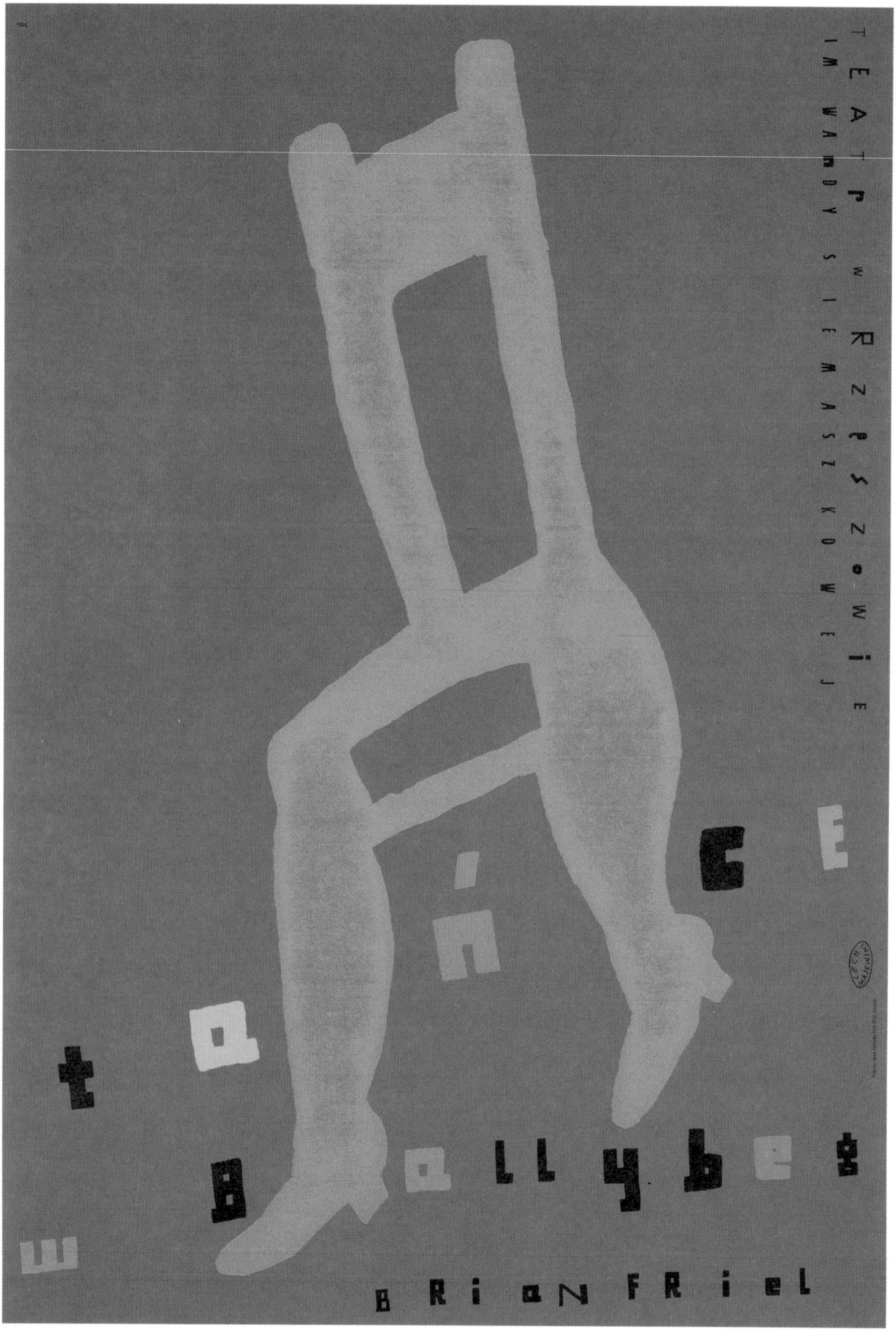

« Dance in Ballybeg ». Poster. 2003. 98 x 68 cm. Offset. Client: Theatre in Rzezow.

Above: « Dance in Ballybeg ». Sketches for the poster. 2003.
Under: « Lovely Money ». 2000. Poster. 98 x 68 cm. Offset. Client: Theatre in Rzeszow.

« Little Prince ». Sketches for the poster. 2003.

« Little Prince ». Poster. 2003. 98 x 68 cm. Offset. Client: Theatre in Rzezow.

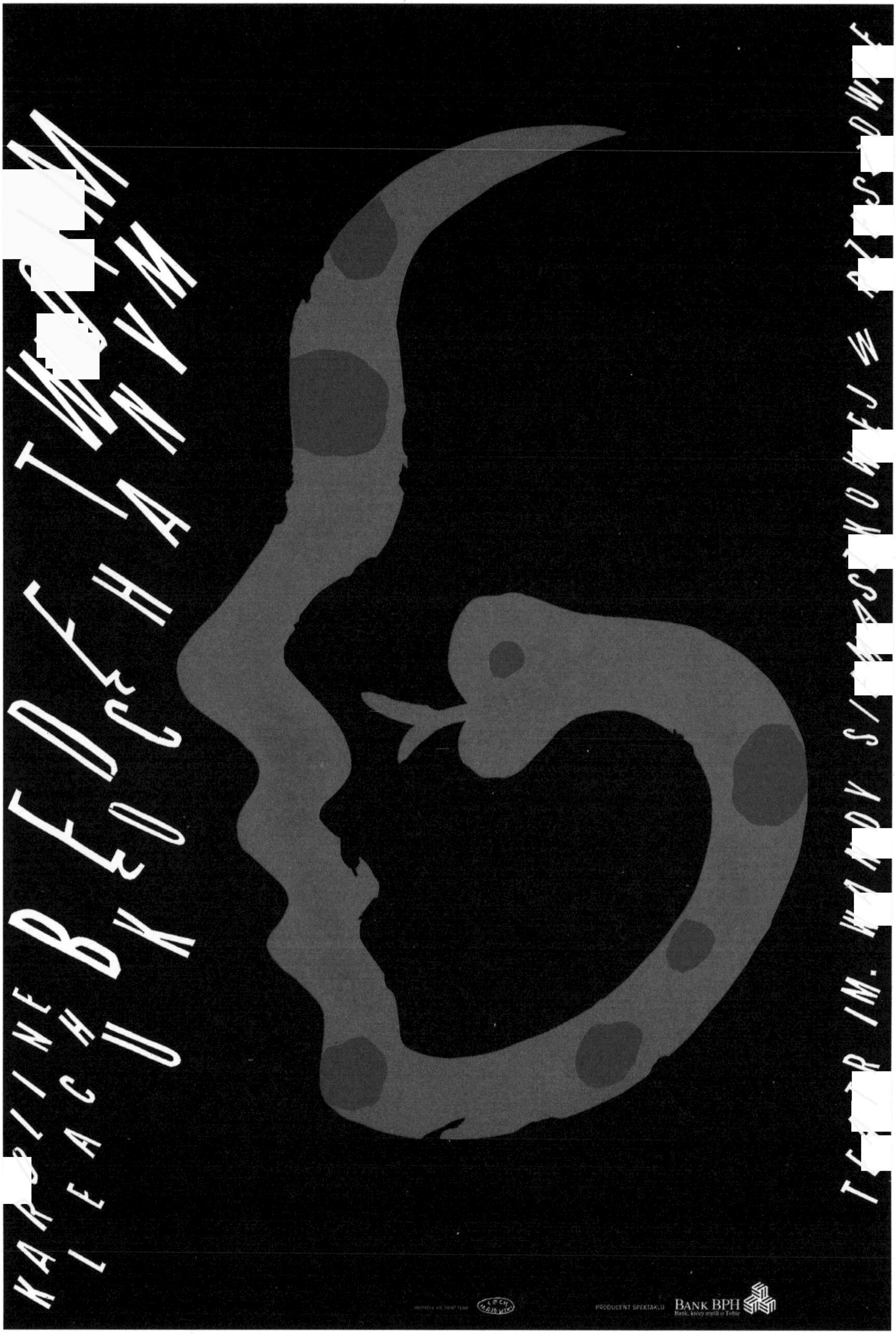

« Mister Love ». Poster. 2000. 98 x 68 cm. Offset. Client: Theatre in Rzezow.

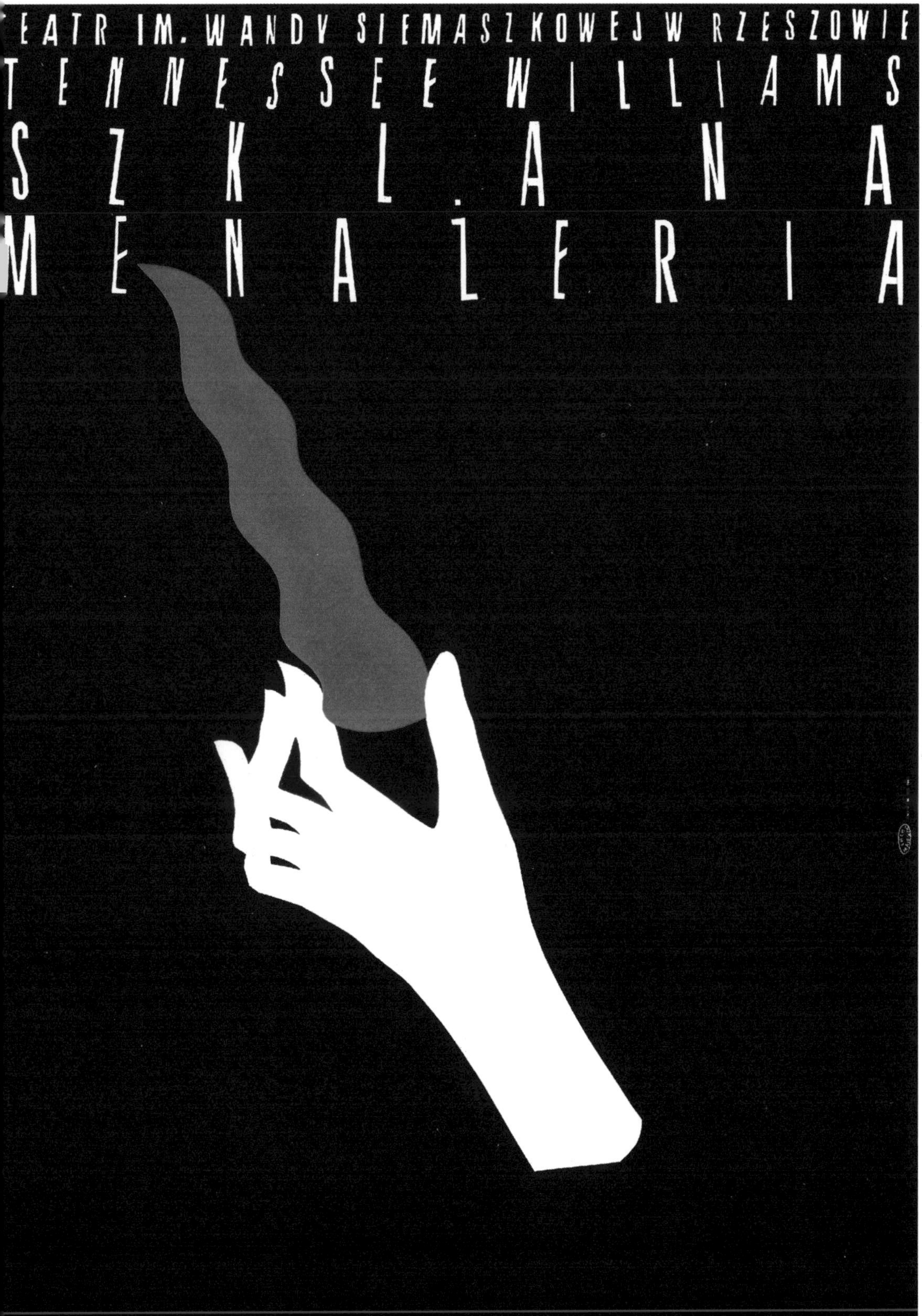

« The Glass Menagerie by T. Williams ». Poster. 2003. 98 x 68 cm. Offset. Client: Theatre in Rzezow.

TEATR IM. WANDY
SIEMASZKOWEJ
W RZESZOWIE
JERZY NIEMCZUK
INKASENT
PRAPREMIERA
POLSKA
PRODUCENCI
GAZETA CODZIENNA
NOWINY

« Collector ». Poster. 2003. 98 x 68 cm. Offset. Client: Theatre in Rzezow.

« Taming of the Screw by Shakespeare ». 2006. Poster. 98 x 68 cm. Offset. Client: Reszow Theatre.

« Dei Popoli Film Festival ». Poster. 2003. 98 x 68 cm. Offset. Client: Film Festival in Florence.

« Echirolles ». 2003. Poster. 98 x 68 cm. Offset. Client: Mois du Graphisme.

Interview with Lech Majewski by Jianping He

1. Why did you choose graphic design as your profession?

I chose graphic design as my profession because I was fascinated with polish poster art. Furthermore, graphic design is a very difficult sphere of art that requires precision of thinking and creativity from the artist. Moreover, a poster immediately reaches the people.

2. How is graphic design present in your life?

Graphic design is very important in my life, but teaching at the Academy of Fine Arts in Warsaw is as well. Moreover, I am organizing the International Poster Biennale in Warsaw.

3. Where does your design inspiration come from?

I am not aware of definite sources of inspiration. The subject is the most important thing for me. Taking into consideration the subject, I choose means which suit my present style and what I like.

4. How many years of graphic training have you received? Do you think the academic education of graphic design is important for a designer?

I've been training for many years. When I was in primary school I attended a painting course. Later I went to the Secondary School of Art. After my secondary education, I studied at the Academy of Fine Arts in Warsaw in professor Henryk Tomaszewski's workshop and with other famous, remarkable Polish graphic designers and painters.

5. Does your own cultural background account for the main influence in your design?

Yes, my graphic design is very subjective; a lot of things shape it, my cultural background as well. Nowadays, only one's own subjective creation can emerge in a contemporary standardized design world.

6. Does literature, theater, music or any other subject contribute to your work?

A lot of fields of art contribute to my work. I am interested in music, theater and film. I think that you can not just be an isolated artist, but have to be a human being.

7. Who would you name as the greatest master of graphic design?

In my opinion, unquestionably the greatest master of graphic design is Henryk Tomaszewski, although there are artists whose creations and attitudes I appreciate a lot.

8. Besides design, what other hobbies do you have?

My hobby besides designing is music. I play the guitar. I used to be a professional musician.

All Men Are Brothers - Designers' Edition - Hesign Publisher

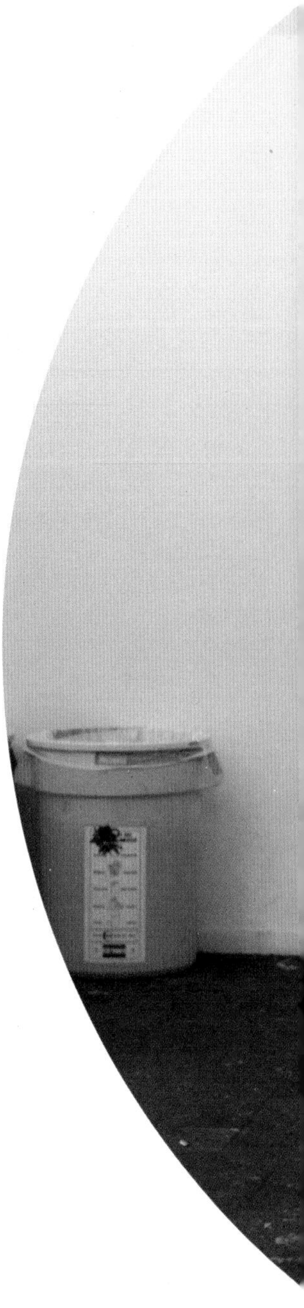

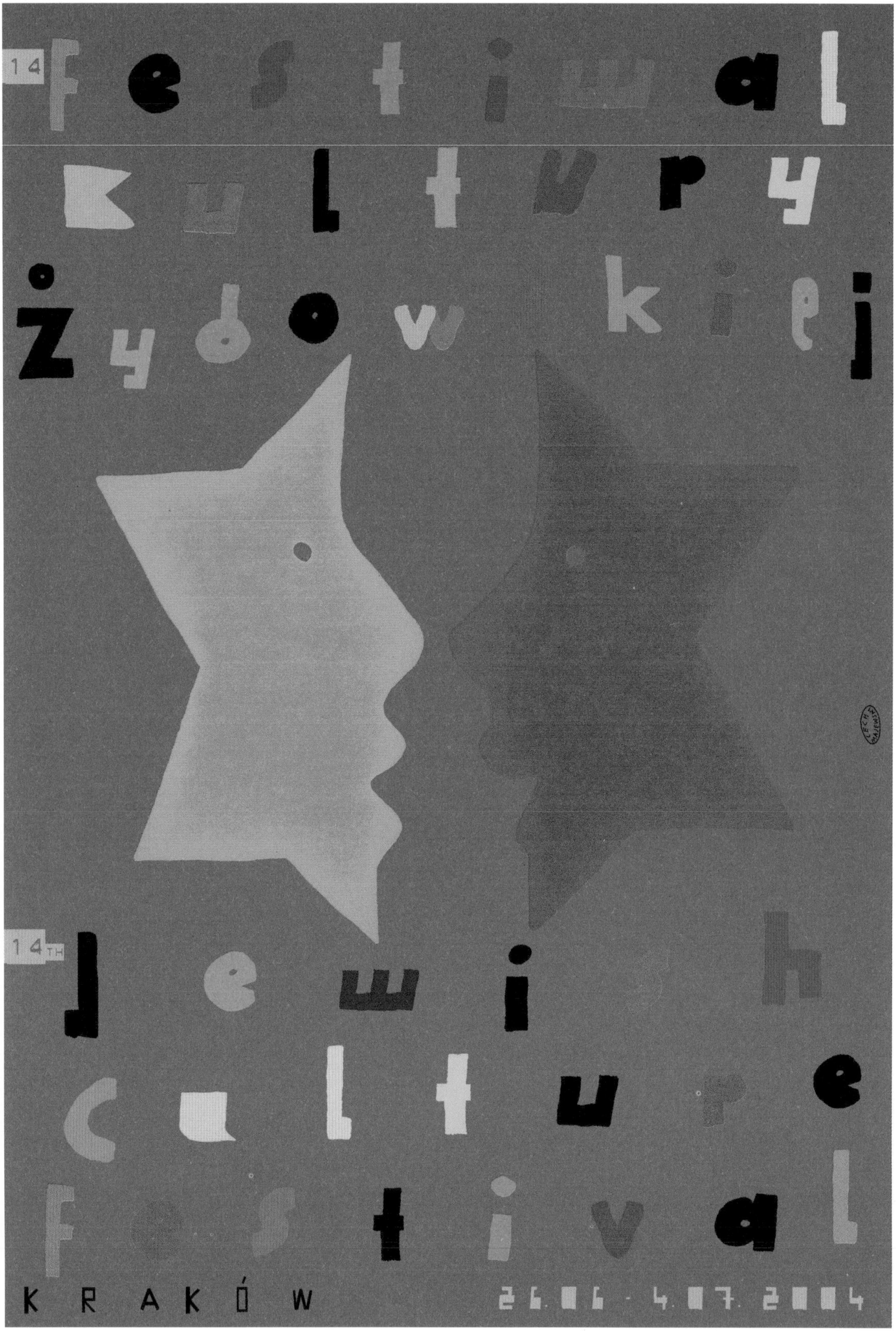

« Jewish Festival ». Poster. 2004. 98 x 68 cm. Offset. Client: Jewish Culture Festival in Cracow.

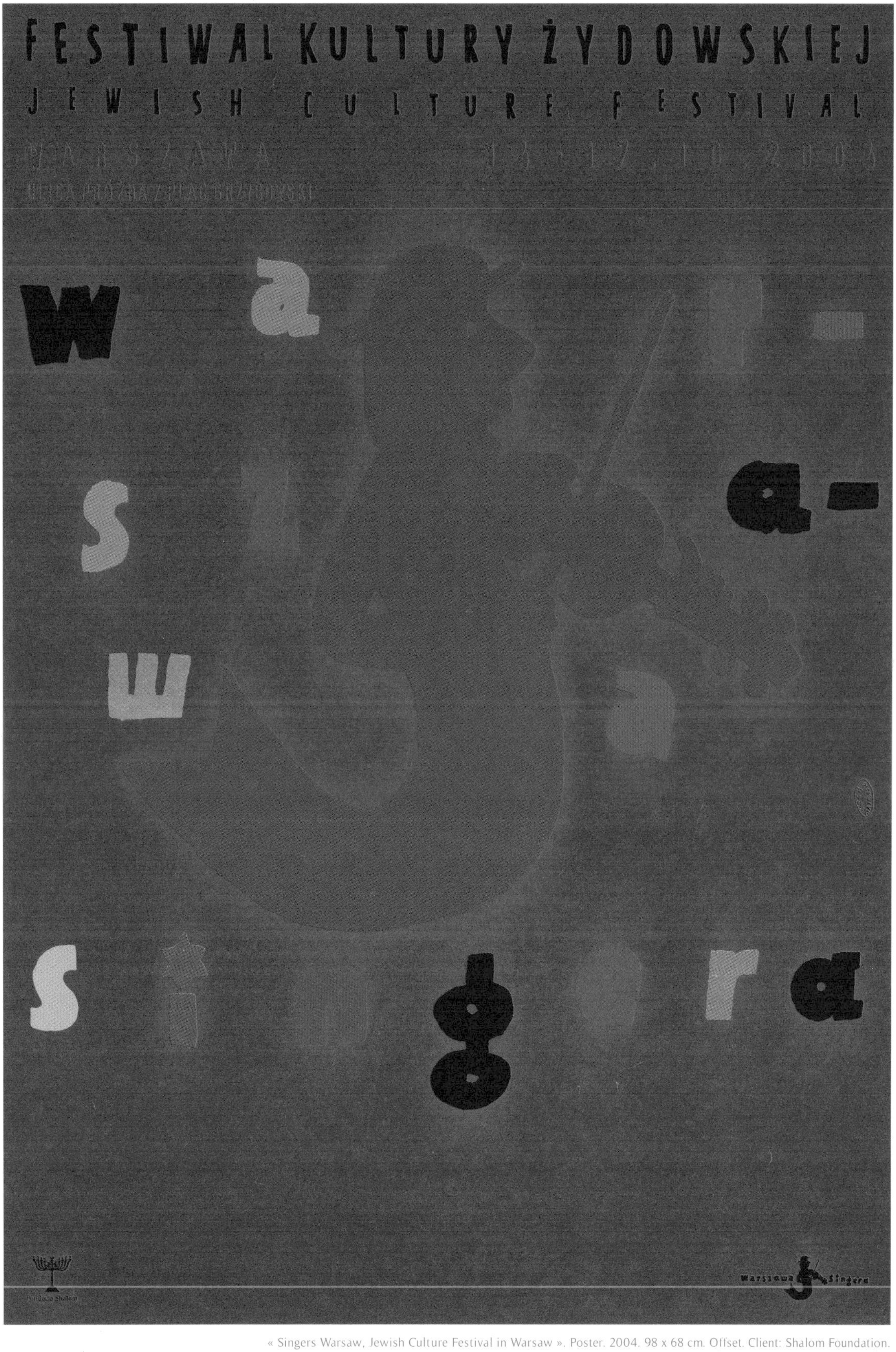

« Singers Warsaw, Jewish Culture Festival in Warsaw ». Poster. 2004. 98 x 68 cm. Offset. Client: Shalom Foundation.

« Motives of the Mask ». Poster. 2000. 98 x 68 cm. Offset.

« Dialogue ». Poster. 2005. 98 x 68 cm. Client: Unesco.

« Dydo Poster Gallery ». Poster. 1999. 98 x 68 cm. Offset. Client: Dido Poster Gallery.

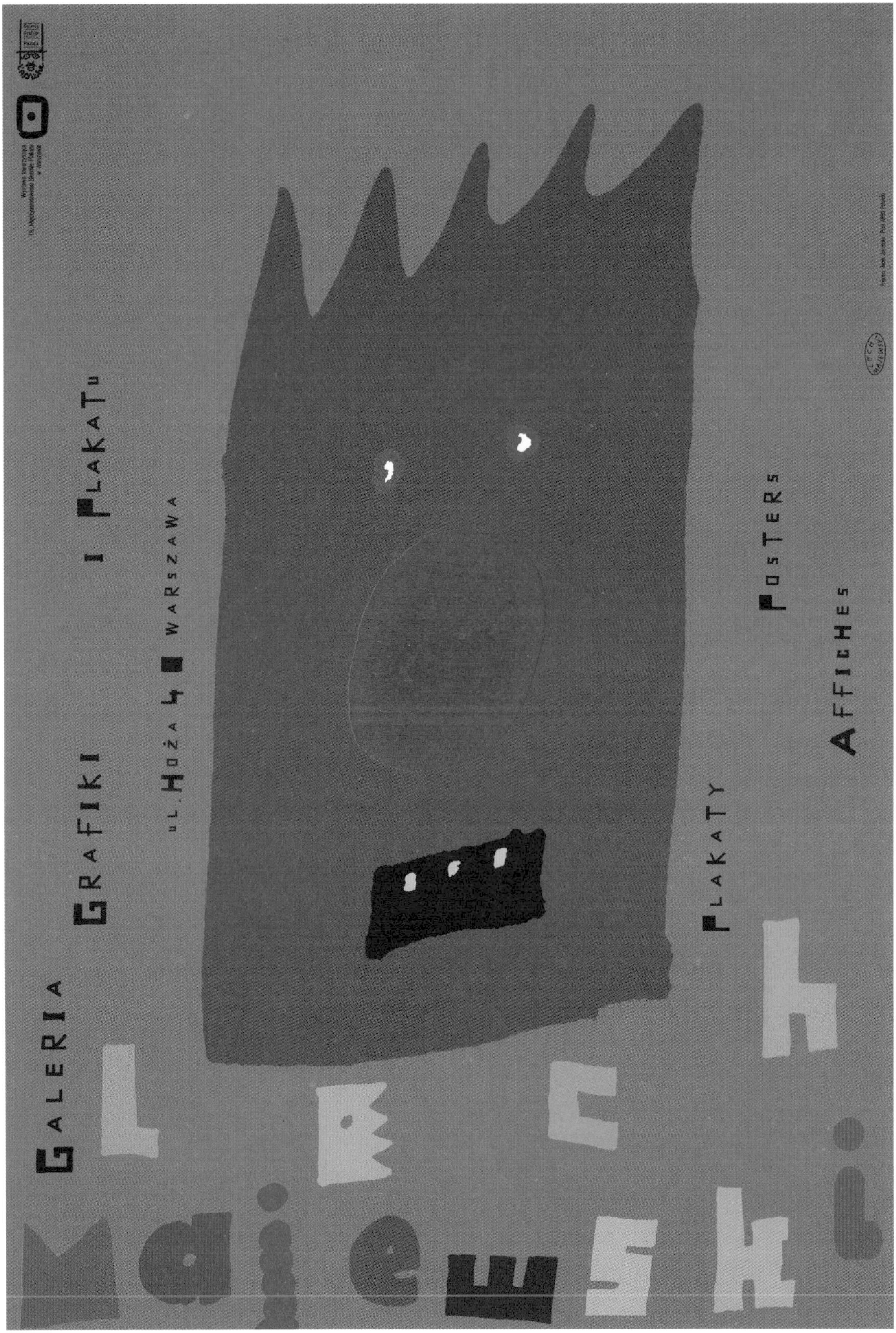

« Lech Majewski Expo ». Poster. 2004. 98 x 68 cm. Offset. Client: Hoza Gallery.

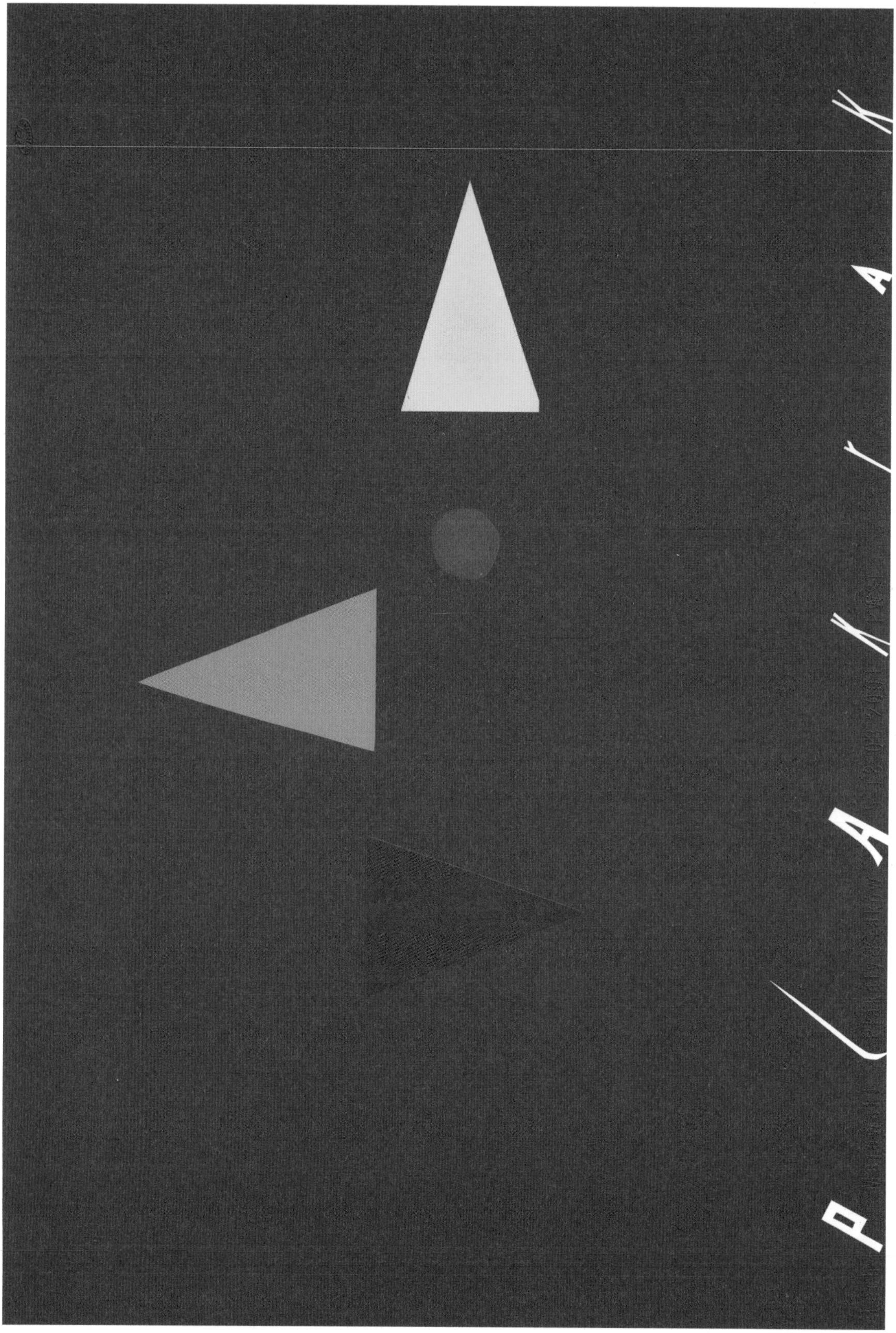

« Lech Majewski Exposition ». Poster. 2001. 98 x 68 cm. Offset. Client: Dydo Gallery in Cracow.

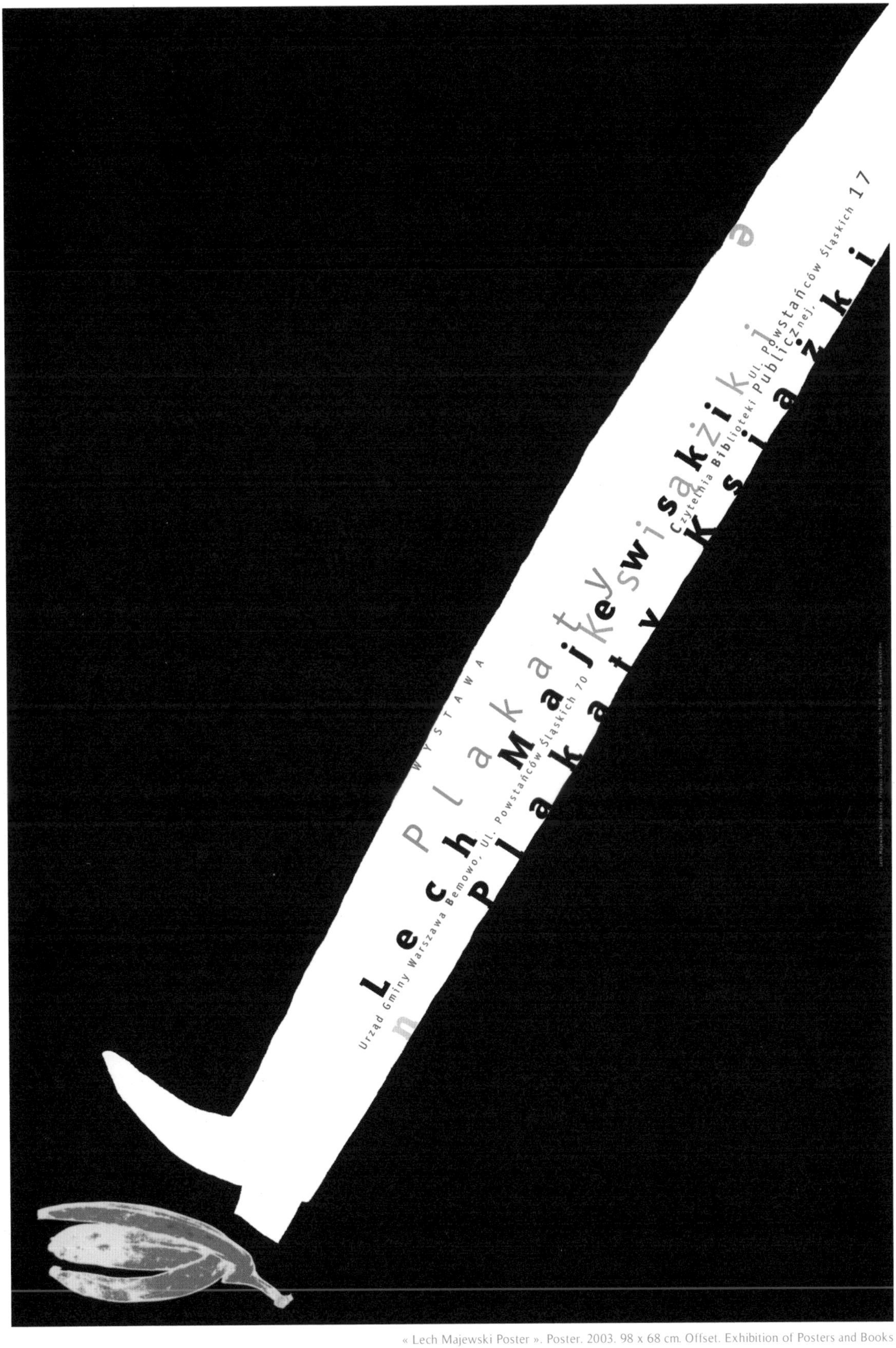

« Lech Majewski Poster ». Poster. 2003. 98 x 68 cm. Offset. Exhibition of Posters and Books

« International Poster Biennale in Warsaw ». Poster. 2006. 98 x 68 cm. Offset. Client: Poster Museum in Warsaw.

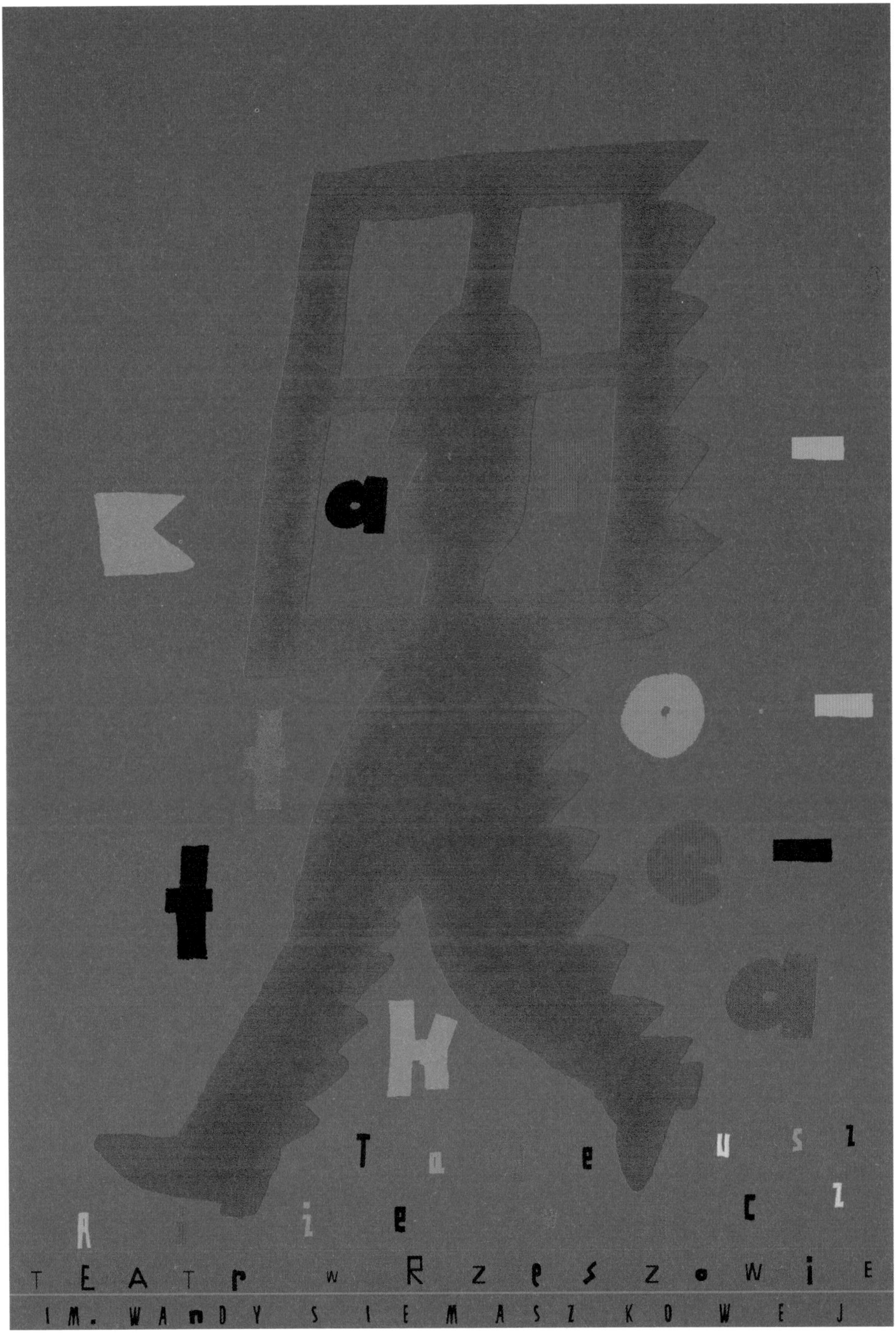

« Kartoteka ». Poster. 2006. 98 x 68 cm. Offset. Client: Siemaszkowa's Rzeszow.

« For thy neighbour, auction ». Poster. 2000. 98 x 68 cm. Offset. Client: Towarzystwo Pomocy Alberta.

« Polish Film Festival ». 2000. Poster. 98 x 68 cm. Offset. Client: Polish Film Festival.

« Polish Radio Festival ». Poster. 2000. 98 x 68 cm. Offset. Client: Polish Radio.

« Polish Radio Festival ». Sketches for the poster. 2000.

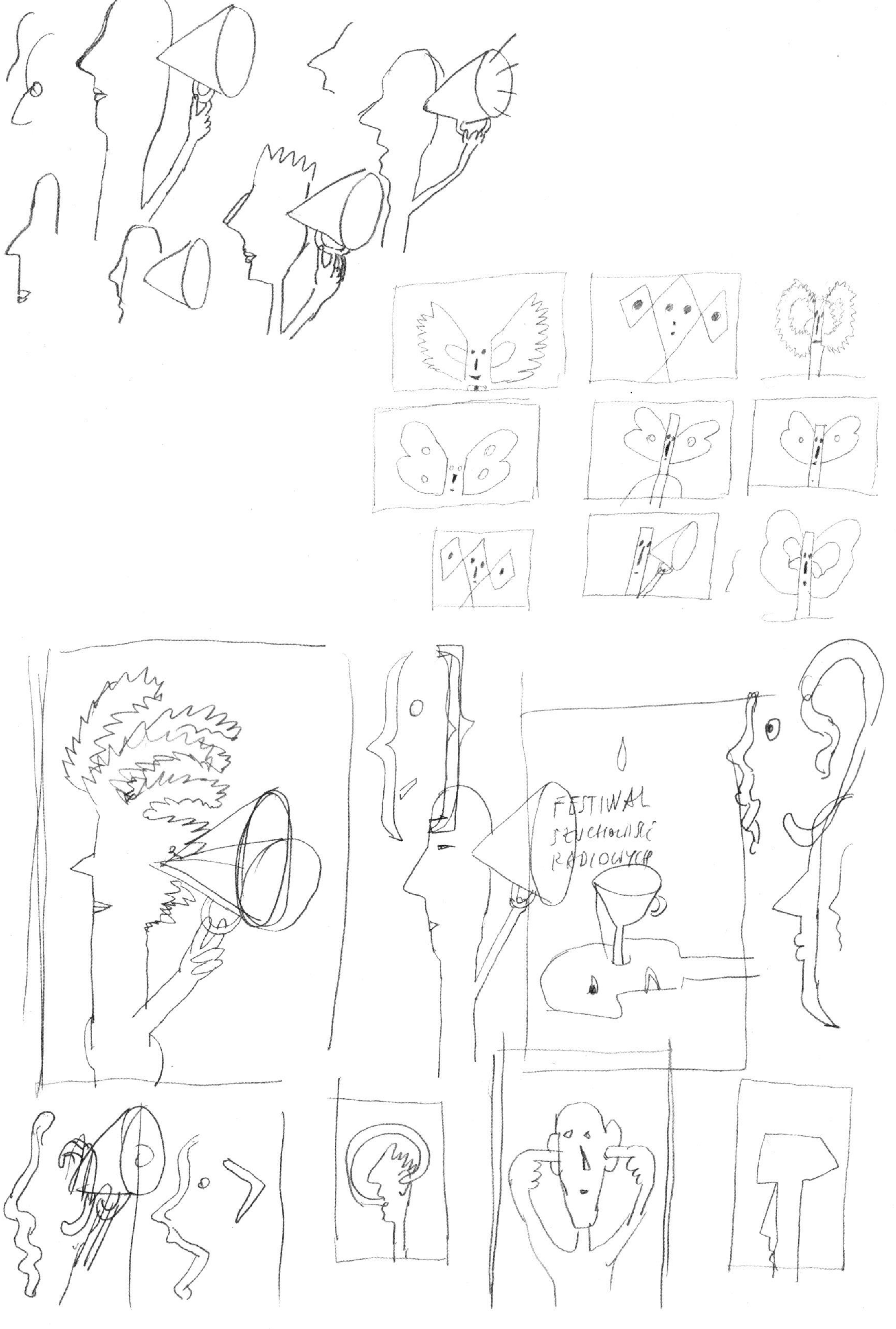

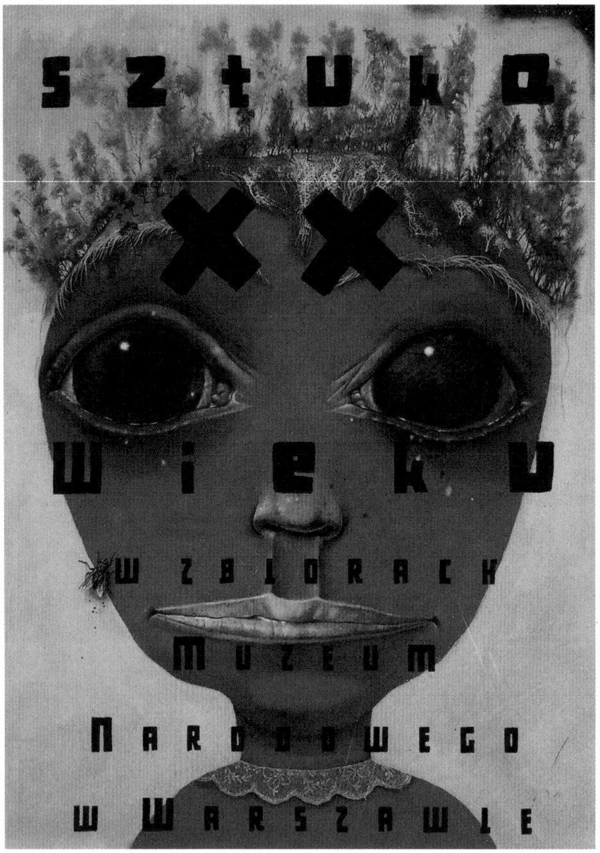

Above: « 20 Century Art ». Poster. 98 x 68 cm. Offset. Contemporary XX Century Art from the collection of the Polish National Museum.
Under: « 23th Polish Film Festival ». Sketches for the poster. 1998.

« 23th Polish Film Festival ». Poster. 1998. 98 x 68 cm. Offset. Client: Polish Film Festival.

STOPSMOG
FUNDACJA OCHRONY POWIETRZA ATMOSFERYCZNEGO
CLEAN AIR FUNDATION

« Stop Smog ». Poster. 98 x 68 cm. Offset. Client: Polish Radio.

« Mother Courage and Her Children ». Poster. 2007. 98 x 68 cm. Offset. Client: Theatre in Rzezow.

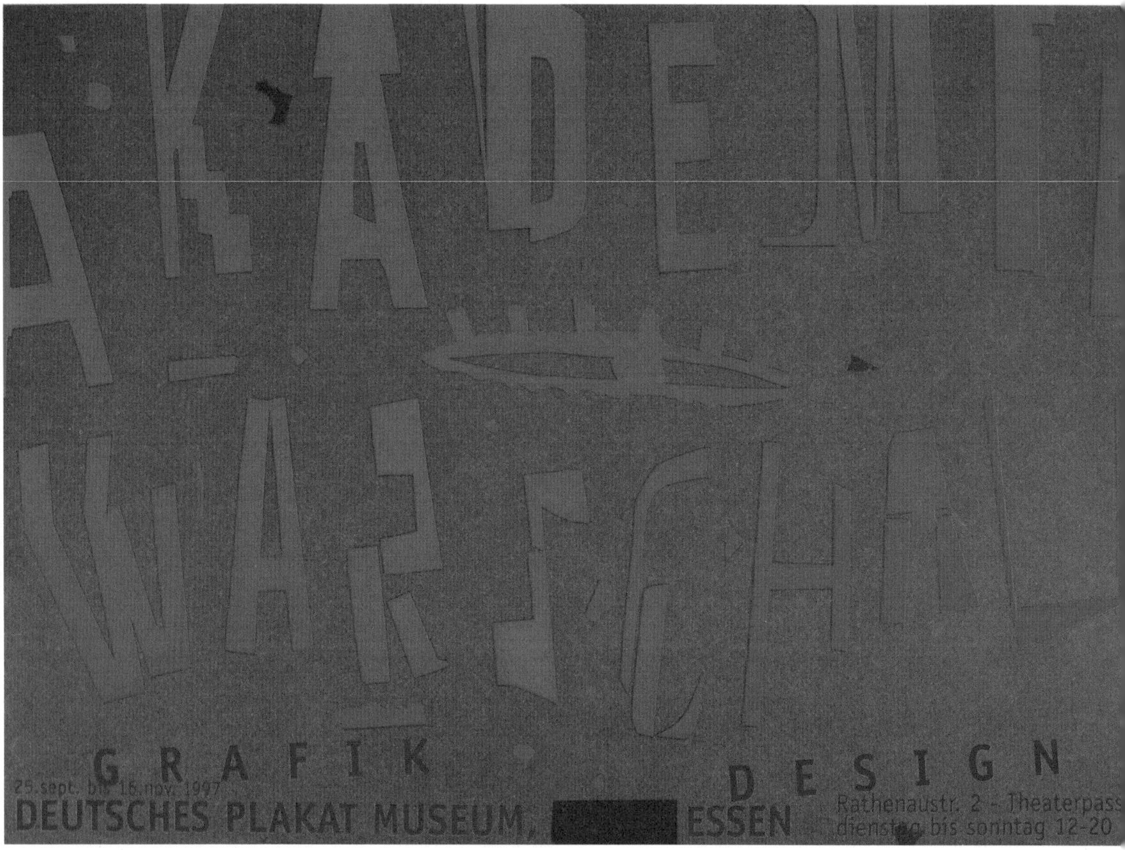

« Academy Warsaw ». Poster. 1997. 68 x 98 cm. Offset. Client: Academy of Fine Arts in Warsaw.

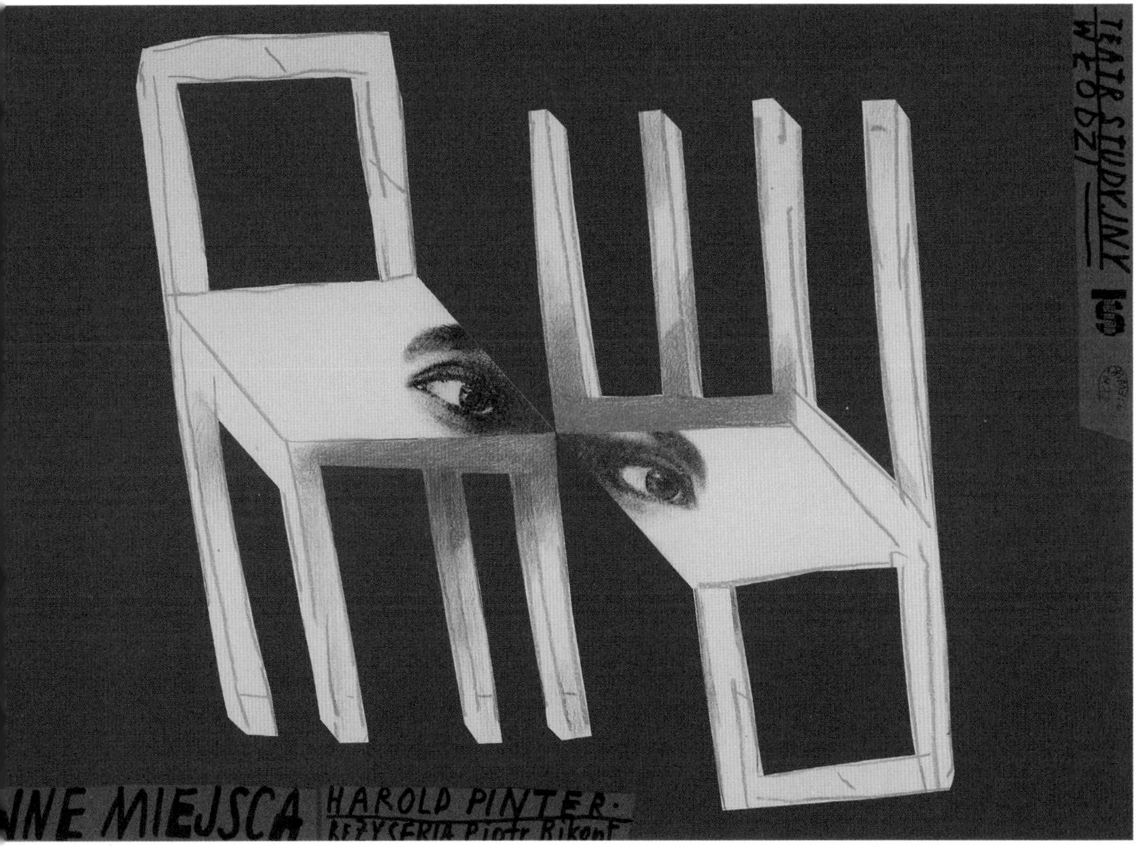

« Other Places, by Harold Pinter ». Poster. 1999. 68 x 98 cm. Offset. Client: "Teatr Studyjny" in Lodz.

« La Locomotora ». Poster. 2002. 68 x 98 cm. Offset. Client: Polish Institut of Mickiewicz.

« Luz de Oriente, Exposition ». Poster. 2002. 68 x 98 cm. Offset. Client: Polish Institut of Mickiewicz.

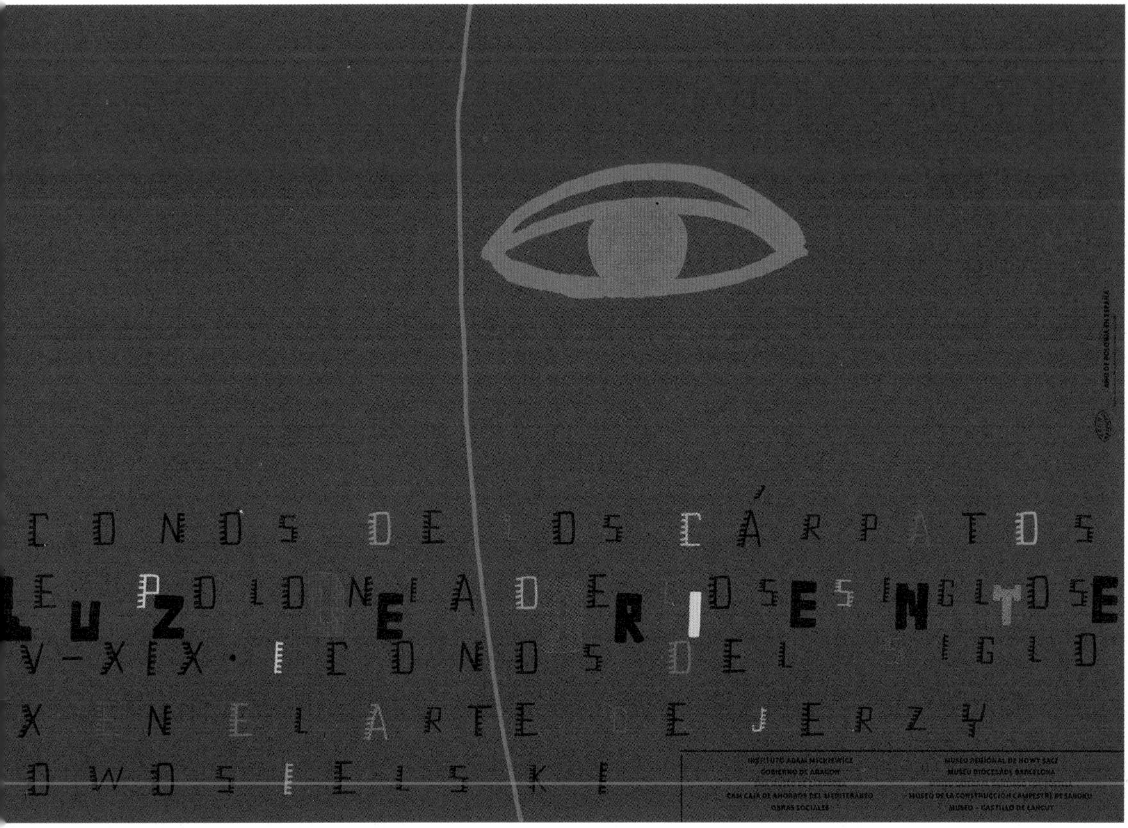

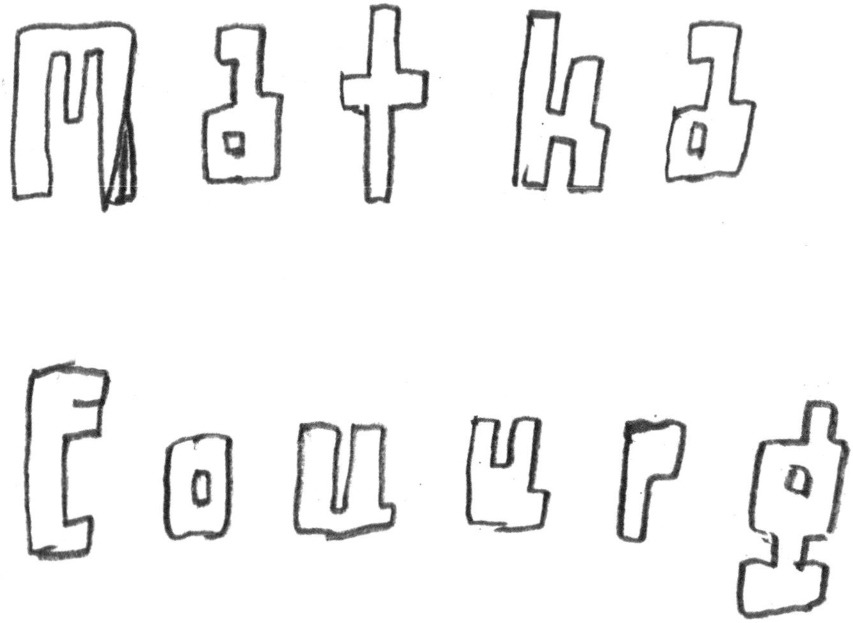

« Mother Courage and Her Children ». Sketch for the poster. 2007.

« In the Opposite Direction » By Omid Rohani

The year 1983 was a dark one in Warsaw. The Communist-controlled government had cracked down on Lech Walesa's 1981 Solidarity movement, and many of its leaders and followers were in prison or in exile. But a subversive splash of color brought life to Warsaw's streets that year - a poster announcing a new theater production of "Historia,"
or "History" by Poland's sardonic 20th-century master, Witold Gombrowicz, which was first uncovered after the author's death in 1969. Featuring a preposterous foot with two finger-like toes held up in a "V," the poster was a complex show of defiance. With its cartoonish surrealism, it seemed to be a call for peace, as well as for victory, and announced that freedom like the play itself would rise from the dead.
Designed by a master of polish graphic art, Henryk Tomaszewski, the "Historia" poster is one of thousands of remarkable posters produced during the country's decades of Communist rule. Made to commemorate or advertise cultural events, they appeared at a time when there was otherwise little or no advertising, and censorship was in full force. The posters (which managed to slip under the censors' radar, as they were more concerned with explicit signs of protest) relieved the gloom of post-war Polish streets, which had remained scarred for decades. "The artists used words like 'flowers' to describe their posters," says Andrea Marks, associate professor in the art department at Oregon State University and founder of "Freedom on the Fence," an online documentary on the history of Polish posters (oregonstate.edu/freedomonthefence). According to Marks the talent of the artists involved and the nurturing personality of Tomaszewski came together to make this movement remarkable.

Known as the "Polish School" of poster art, the movement began after the death of Soviet premier Joseph Stalin in 1953 which allowed for a thawing throughout the Soviet block. Characterized by highly unusual, often grotesque, imagery, the school flourished until the fall of Communism in 1989. Many experts agree that an artistic high-point was reached in the 1960s, when the movement's name came into use, and graphic artists throughout Europe made pilgrimages to Poland to study under Tomaszewski who was then a professor of design at Warsaw's Academy of Fine Arts. In recent years, the Polish Poster School has established itself as a small, but growing niche market for collectors, who may have discovered the movement while traveling in Eastern Europe, or by browsing and buying on the internet. "The past year has been the best I have ever had in terms of polish theater posters," says Martin Rosenberg, a Santa Fe, New Mexico, poster dealer and curator (www.mrposter.com). The Polish poster was an "explosion in design" that produced the most inventive graphic style to emerge from Communist-controlled Eastern Europe, says Jim Aulich, author of "Political Posters in Central and Eastern Europe, 1945-95." Theater posters are significant to the movement because of the role that theater itself played in Communist-era Polish society, says theater historian Tomasz Kubikowski. Theater was a forum where actors, directors and audiences could "express opinions, and, more importantly, emotions that could not find other ways of coming out," he says.

In contrast to the official style of socialist realism in painting and sculpture and the graphic style of official government posters, the posters created by artists in the Polish School of Poster movement functioned as sly commentaries on Poland's political situation and provided opportunities for individual expression, says Maria Kurpik, director of the Wilanow Poster Museum in Warsaw (www.postermuseum.pl).

For collectors now, Polish film posters are a bigger draw (in March, Waldemar Swierzy's 1973 poster for the movie "Midnight Cowboy" sold for GBP 960 ($1,810), double its estimated value in 1996, says Sarah Hodgson, head of the department for popular entertainment at Christie's in London). Nevertheless, Polish theater posters hold a special place for collectors, says Donald Mayer, whose New York gallery and website, Contemporary Posters, specializes in polish poster art (www.contemporary posters.com). Mr. Mayer and his wife, Ylain, started out collecting abstract expressionist art from the 1950s and 1960s, which led to an interest in polish poster art from the same period. Like their customers, the Mayers were drawn to the dramatic stories behind many of the theater posters. "It's the history as well as the art that fascinates us," Mrs. Mayer says. For instance, "Dziady," or "Forefathers," a 19th century play by Adam Mickiewicz, is a humanistic plea for freedom that was banned during Poland's Stalinist years. In late 1967, a revival at Warsaw's Teatr Norodowy came under the eye of censors for drawing too close a connection between the czarist tyrants of the play and Poland's Communist government.

In March 1968, after the production was banned, students marched in protest from the theater to a Mickiewicz memorial, triggering a wave of national unrest. The poster, designed by Roman Cieslewicz, a polish emigre working in France at that time, was hardly seen on the streets, but it proved interesting. Featuring a stone man about to crumble into pieces, and a hole where his heart should be, the poster brilliantly dramatizes the predicament of a society on the brink of collapse. At Contemporary Posters, the poster Cieslewicz is priced at $375.

In a famous poster designed in 1962 by Franciszek Starowieyski for Friedrich Durrenmatt's play, "Frank V," a skull is grafted onto a baroque palace, and the cavity where the nose would have been is an open window (It is priced at 400 € ($512) at the Polish Poster Gallery, www.poster.com.pl , in Warsaw's Old Town.).

Uwe Loesch, a Dusseldorf poster artist, whose work - like Tomaszewski's - is in the design collection at New York's Museum of Modern Art, says such strange and even morbid figures are one of the features that distinguish the Polish theater posters. "There are historic reasons for the monsters," says Uwe Loesch, who sees a cathartic power in the images. "Poland was completely destroyed after the war. Most of the concentration camps were in Poland. Then came the dictatorship of the Poland's arch enemy, Russia. The Poles were traumatized."

After Communism's fall, the streets of Polish cities were filled with Western advertising, and with Western tourists. Piotr Syrycki, an employee at the Polish Poster Gallery, credits Western tourists with helping to rediscover the Polish poster school. Increased travel by Poles also has played a role. Ms. Marks learned about the movement from books brought by a student who came to Oregon from Warsaw as part of an exchange program in 1997. "As soon as I saw these books, I was floored," she says.

Originally produced in print runs of around 3,000, Polish theater posters from the Communist era were printed on low-quality paper. The Mayers put the fragile pieces on to a linen backing. Their advice to collectors is to rely on reputable dealers to distinguish between originals and reprints. It is also important to look closely at the texture of the paper, the color of the images and the publisher logos. Jan Lenica's famous poster for the opera "Wozzeck" is at the high-end of prices for the theater poster genre. Inspired by Alban Berg's modernist opera, the poster recalls the expressionist styles of the 1920s, (when Berg's opera premiered), while the colors anticipate the psychedelic hues of the 1970s. The poster won a gold medal for "posters promoting culture and art" at Warsaw's first International Poster Biennial in 1966, at the height of the Polish poster school. The original 1964 version now costs 1,200 euros at the Polish Poster Gallery and $850 at Contemporary Posters in New York. However, the Polish Poster Gallery exhibits a "Historia" bought for a modest 120 €-150 €.

The 20th Poster Biennial, held at the Wilanow Poster Museum, is on now through Sept. 17. This year's most acclaimed theater poster, awarded a prize at the Biennial by the Polish Stage Artists' Union, is by Lech Majewski, a professor of graphic arts at the Warsaw Academy of Fine Arts. His poster for "Balladyna," a mid-19th century Romantic drama by Juliusz Slowacki, features a stencil-like image of a woman and a blackout line of a knife. It recalls the menacing, figurative tradition of the Polish school, but uses new typefaces and color schemes.

"It is important for the graphic designer to look back as well as look into the future," says Lech Majewski.

« Mother Courage and Her Children ». Sketch for the poster. 2007.

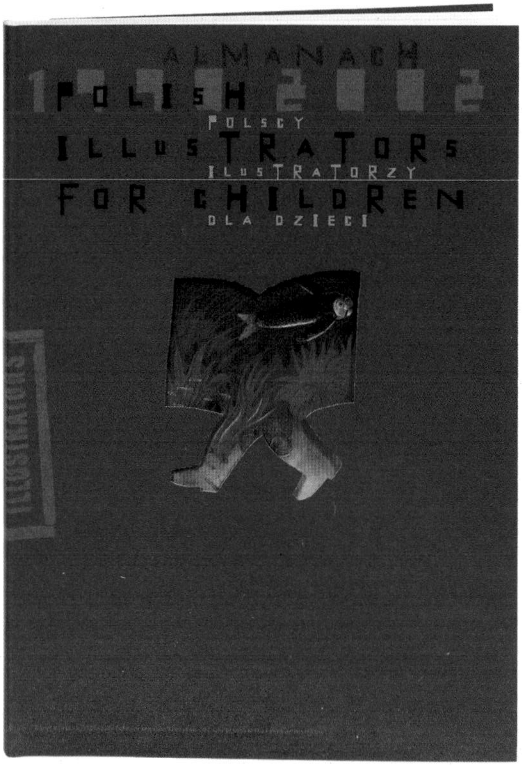

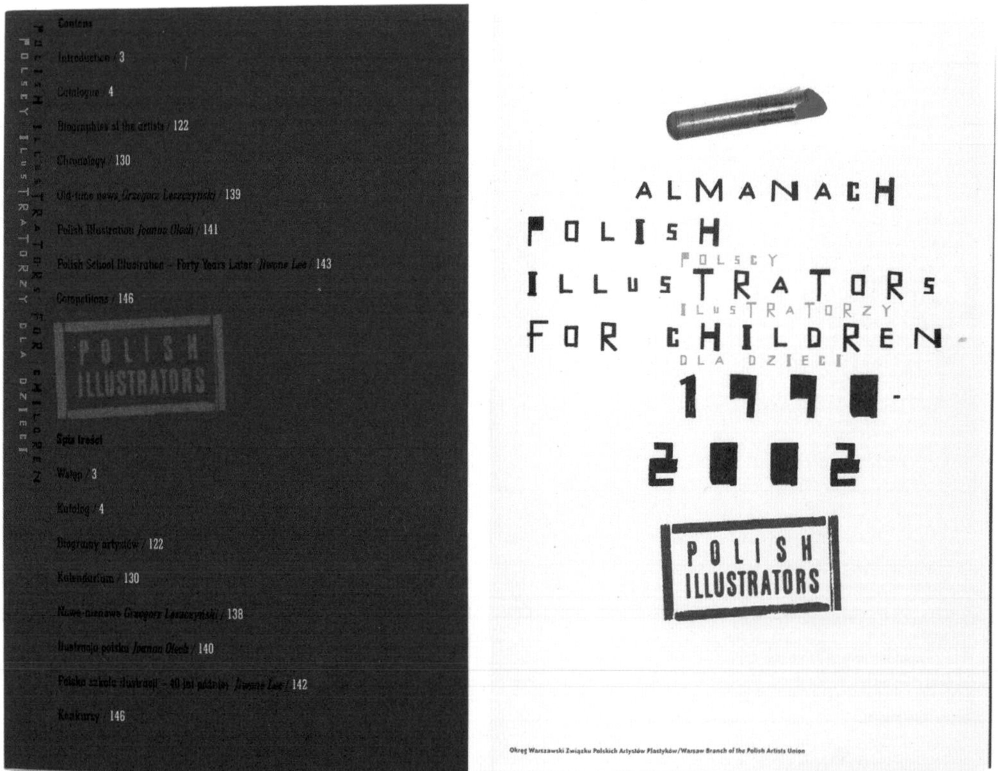

« Almanach » Book and cover.

« Mother Courage and Her Children ». Sketch for the poster. 2007.

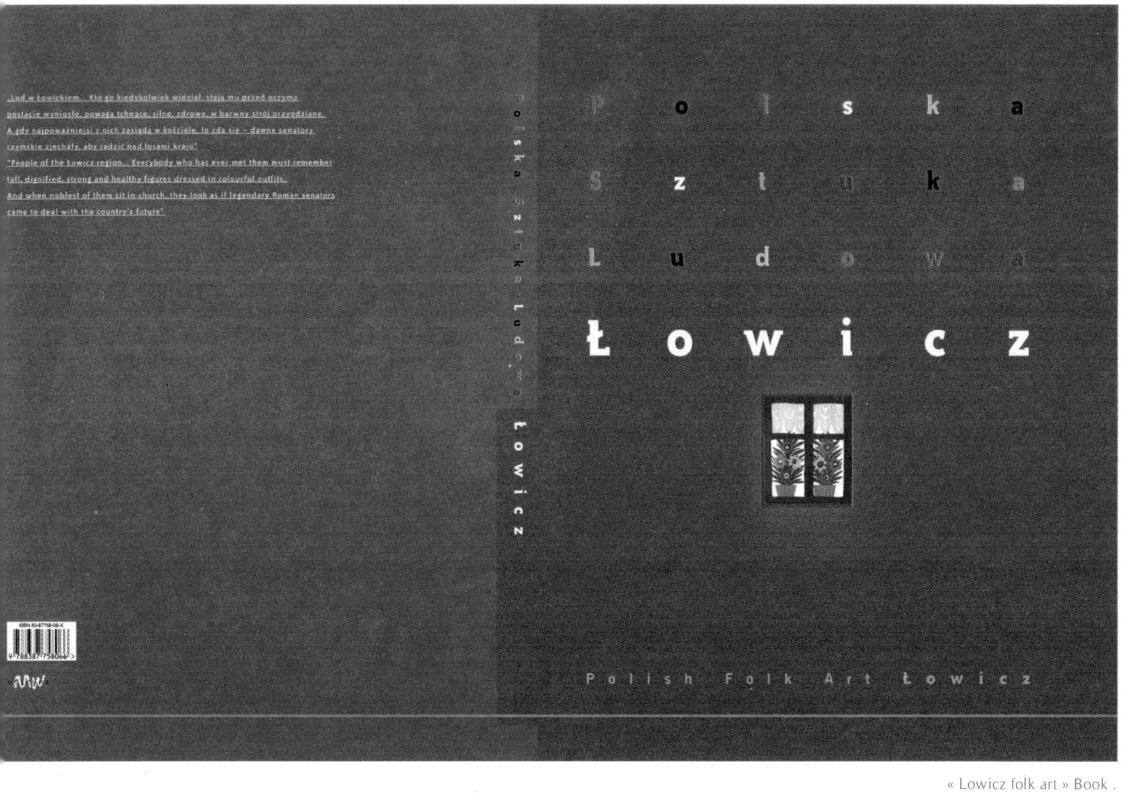

„Lud w Łowickiem... Kto go kiedykolwiek widział, stają mu przed oczyma
postacie wyniosłe, powagą tchnące, silne, zdrowe, w barwny strój przyodziane.
A gdy najpoważniejsi z nich zasiądą w kościele, to zda się – dawne senatory
rzymskie zjechały, aby radzić nad losami kraju"
"People of the Łowicz region... Everybody who has ever met them must remember
tall, dignified, strong and healthy figures dressed in colourful outfits.
And when noblest of them sit in church, they look as if legendary Roman senators
came to deal with the country's future"
Polska Sztuka Ludowa Łowicz
Polska
Sztuka
Ludowa
Łowicz
Polish Folk Art Łowicz

« Lowicz folk art » Book .

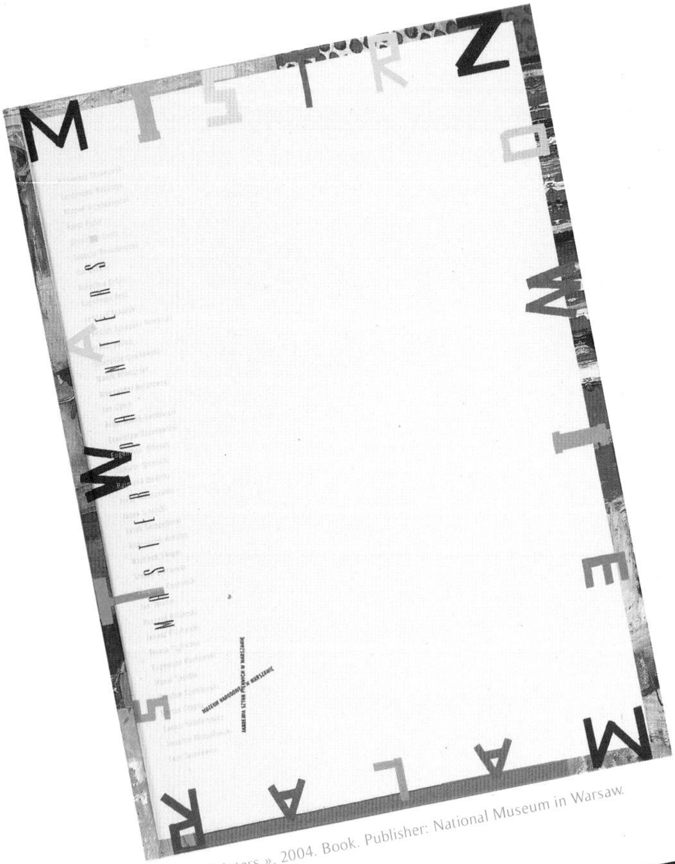

« Master Painters ». 2004. Book. Publisher: National Museum in Warsaw.

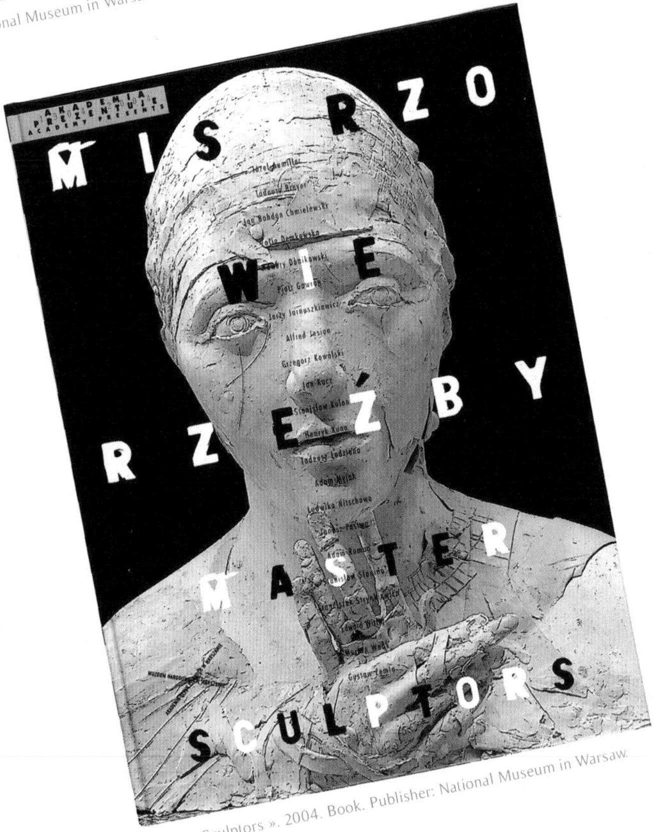

« Master Sculptors ». 2004. Book. Publisher: National Museum in Warsaw.

« Masters of graphic art ». 2004. Book. Publisher: National Museum in Warsaw.

« Picasso Cover ». 2004. Book. Publisher: National Museum in Warsaw.

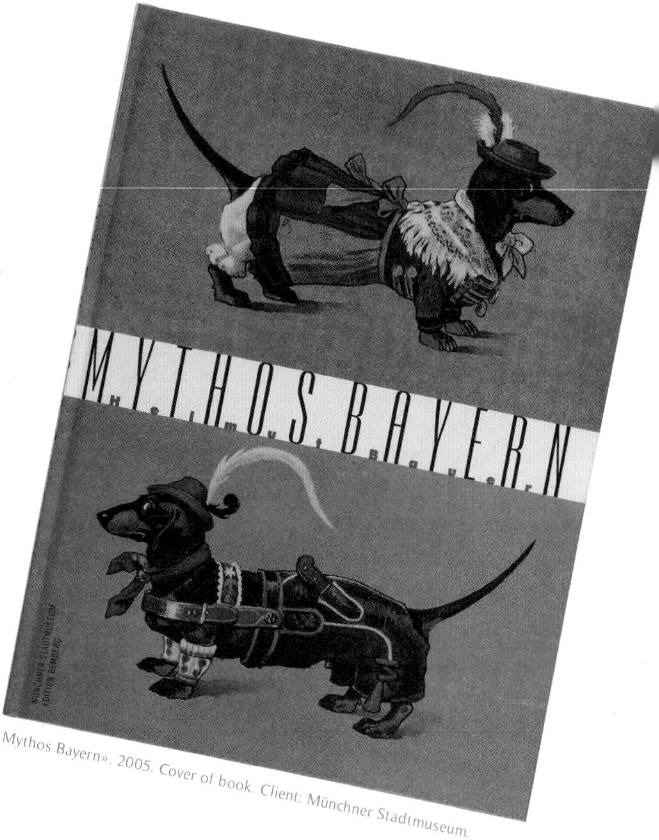

« Mythos Bayern». 2005. Cover of book. Client: Münchner Stadtmuseum.

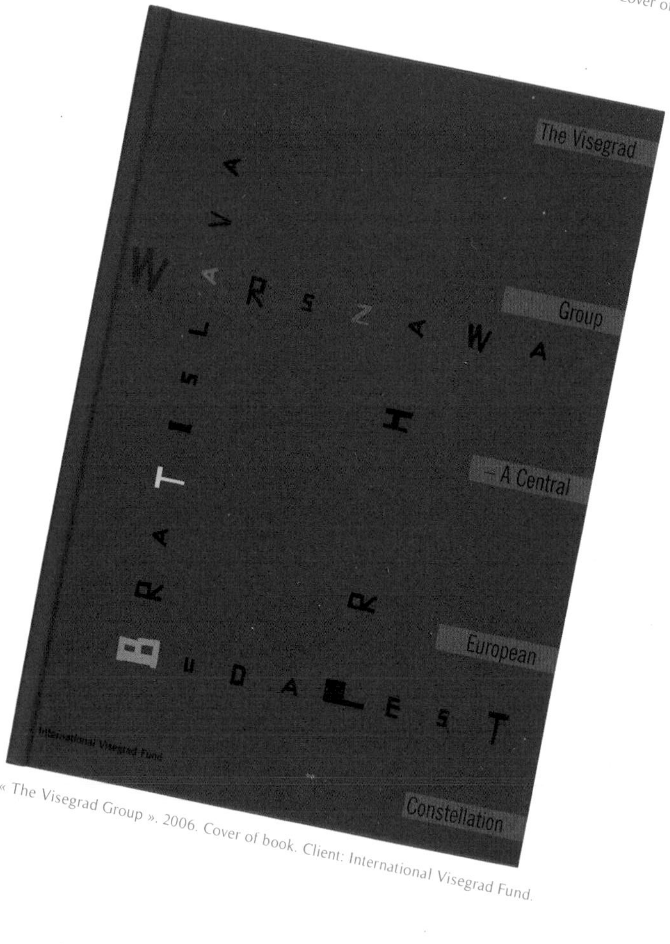

« The Visegrad Group ». 2006. Cover of book. Client: International Visegrad Fund.

« Paul Klee. From a scetchbook to the painting ». 2000. Book. Client: Polish National Museum in Warsaw.

« Schwabing ». Book. Publisher: "Stadtmuseum in München".

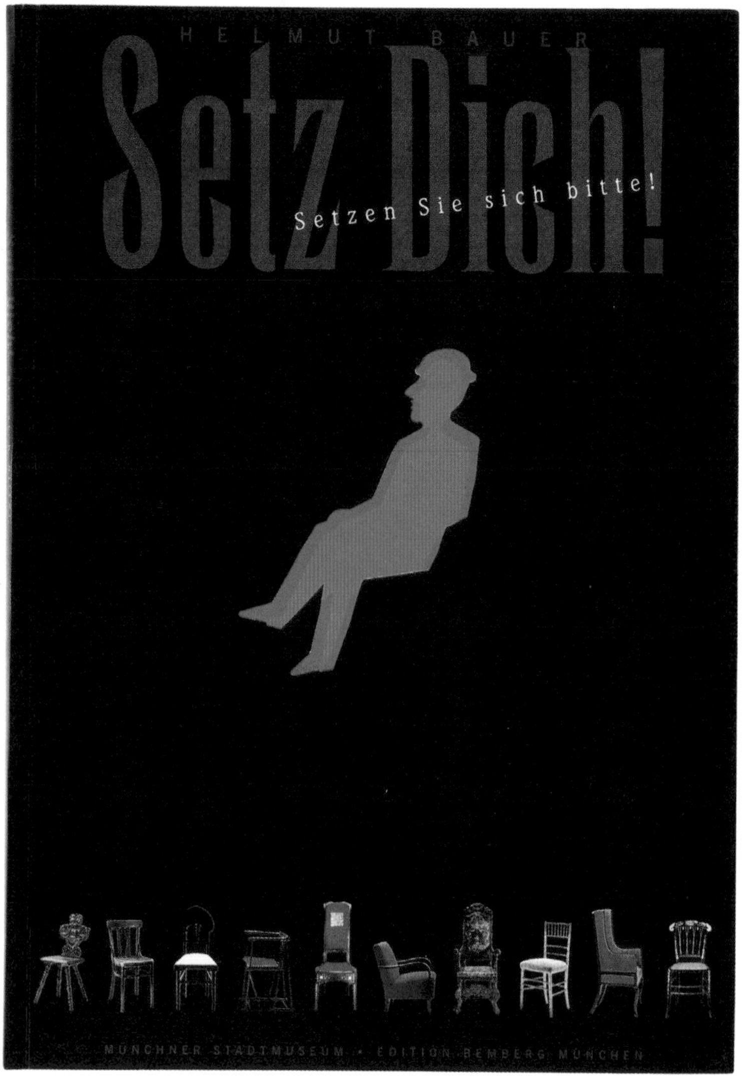

« Setz Dich ». Book and cover. Publisher: "Stadtmuseum in München".

Maupo kayo!
Istuudu!
Ülj le!
बस्नोस
Mohon duduk!

Setz Dich!
Gestaltung LECH MAJEWSKI
HELMUT BAUER
MÜNCHNER STADTMUSEUM
EDITION BEMBERG MÜNCHEN

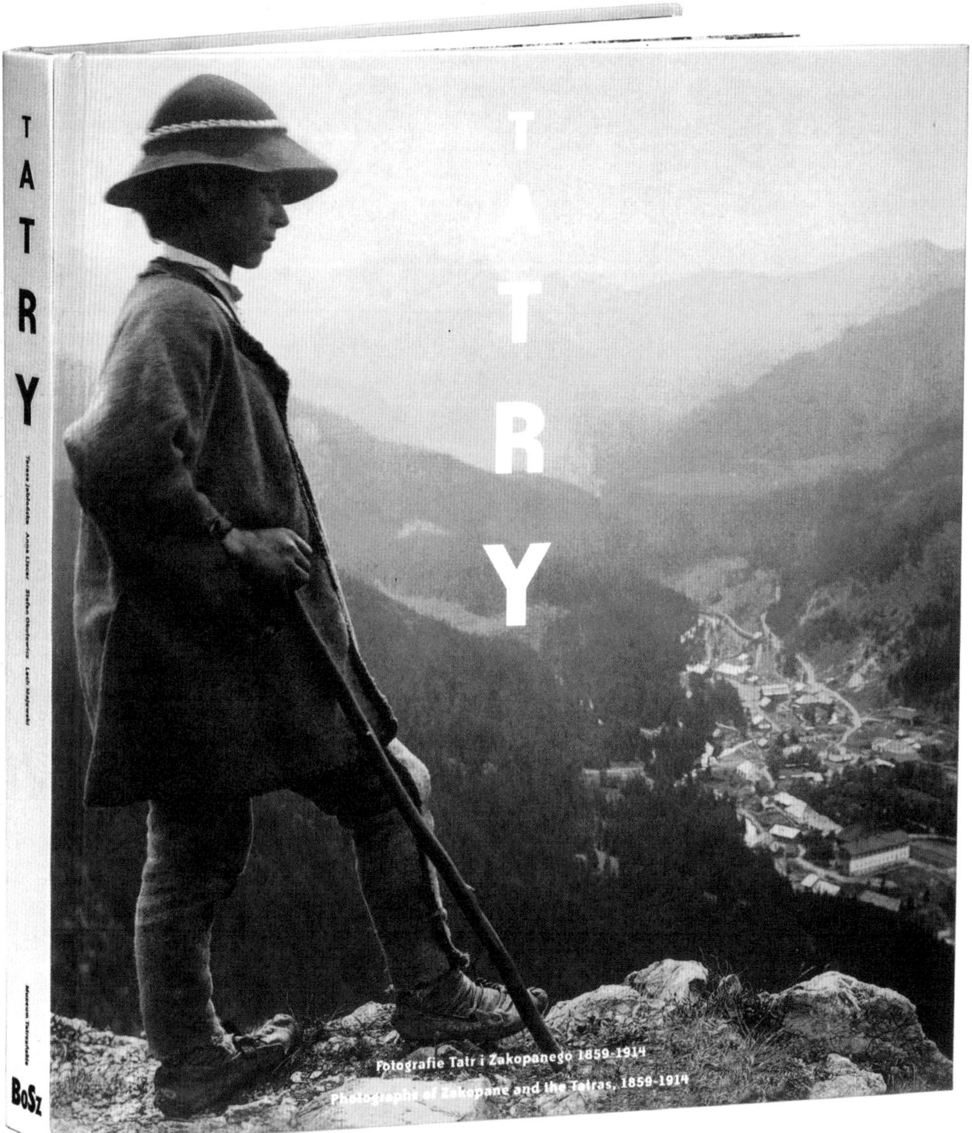

« Tarty ». Book and cover. Publisher: BOSZ.

że ich ujęcia nie stworzyły obligatoryjnej, jak w wypadku Morskiego Oka na przykład, konwencji ich widzenia i przedstawiania. Postrzegając więc te „reglowe" fascynacje dawnych fotografików zauważyć warto, że za sprawą Awita Szuberta pewnego rodzaju artystycznego awansu doczekała się Dolina Chochołowska, *de facto* w malarstwie i literaturze zupełnie w ich czasach nieobecna, że krajobrazowe wartości Doliny Małej Łąki także po raz pierwszy ujawnione zostały za sprawą Stanisława Bizańskiego i Walerego Eljasza w czasach, gdy nikt o niej nie pisał i nikt jej nie malował. Co ciekawe, to samo odnieść można i do Gęsiej Szyi: rozległe ujęcia krajobrazowe wykonane z niej w latach 1876-1878 stanowią swoiste odkrycie krajobrazowe i wręcz inicjują kult roztaczającego się z niej widoku, uznawanego za jeden z najwspanialszych z północnej strony Tatr.

Mówiąc o tych zjawiskach warto jednak zauważyć także, iż stosunkowo wcześnie fotografia tatrzańska zdradzać poczęła swe aspiracje bardziej wysokogórskie i w stosunku do niejednego z górskich obiektów znów wyprzedzała literaturę i malarstwo. Dotyczy to nie tylko Doliny Białej Wody czy Doliny Kaczej, ale także krajobrazowych ujęć prawdziwie już wysokogórskich, takich jak Awita Szuberta widok z Krzyżnego (1876-1878), sfotografowany przez niego w czasie, gdy nie istniało jeszcze ani jedno jego malarskie ujęcie i gdy nie doczekał się on jeszcze literackiego opisu. Takich zaś szczegółów przytoczyć by tu można więcej, ale już tu wykazane wskazują dowodnie, iż już w ostatnim ćwierćwieczu XIX stulecia fotografia tatrzańska zyskała swą autonomiczność i odnalazła swe miejsce w rodzinie sztuk zajmujących się Tatrami.

Jeśli się tu doda, że niejedno z prezentowanych w niniejszym albumie zdjęć reprezentuje bardzo wysoki poziom artystyczny, że niektórzy fotograficy czynnie dokumentowali różne dokonania taternickie i ważne zjawiska kulturowe, wówczas okaże się jasno, iż dawna fotografia o tematyce tatrzańskiej, zakopiańskiej i góralskiej zajmuje autentycznie ważne miejsce w dziejach znaczenia Tatr i Podhala dla kultury polskiej.

1 J. Krzyżanowski, *Folklor Podhala w literaturze*, „Literatura Ludowa", 1932, nr 1, s. 5.
2 J. Młodziejowski, *Góry polskie w polskiej muzyce* [w:] Sympozjum „Góry w kulturze polskiej", Kraków 9-10 listopada 1974 r., Kraków 1975, s. 35.
3 Zob. W.A. Wójcik, *Słowo wstępne* [w:] *Góry polskie w malarstwie. Materiały z sympozjum*, Kraków 4 grudnia 1998, pod red. W.A. Wójcika, Kraków 1999, s. 6-7.
4 Tamże, s. 6.
5 G. Niewiadomy, *Krajobraz z góralem. Tatry i Podhale w sztuce polskiej 1836-1945. Tom I. Tatry romantyczne 1836-1889*, Gdańsk 1995, s. 32.
6 G. Niewiadomy, *Gdy o Tatrach mało kto wiedział... Najstarsze pejzaże tatrzańskie od Van den Blocka do Głowackiego* [w:] *Góry polskie w malarstwie. Materiały z sympozjum*, Kraków 4 grudnia 1998, pod red. W.A. Wójcika, Kraków 1999, s. 10.
7 Zjawisko to charakteryzuje G. Niewiadomy, op. cit., s. 330.

cited clearly show that by the last quarter of the 19th century photography had won an autonomous place among the arts which addressed Tatran subjects.

If we remember that many of the photographs presented in this album are of a very high quality artistically and that some of the early photographers took an active part in the documentation of a variety of both climbing exploits and cultural phenomena – it will be clear beyond all doubt that the early Tatran photography, on subjects connected with Zakopane and the Gorale Highlanders, commands a position of indisputable significance in the history of the Tatras and the Podhale region and their contribution to Polish culture.

W Zakopanem zbiera się wśród lata wprawdzie nieliczne, ale za to dobrańsze niż gdzie indziej towarzystwo. Przyjeżdżają tu ludzie głównie dla zwiedzenia gór lub wytchnienia umysłowego, ci zaś, co szukają zabawy, interesów, odgrywania jakich tonów, choroby na panów, marnowania majątku jadą do kąpieli, Tatry dla nich dziką pustynią. (...) Spotykając w Zakopanem nieraz wśród znakomitości artystycznych, literackich różnych zawodów i wszelkich odcieni wymoczków salonowych śledziłem przyczynę pojawienia się takich okazów na jałowym dla nich gruncie; badania przekonały mnie o istnieniu mody, o warunkach dobrego tonu zajrzenia chociaż raz w Tatry, które się im barbarzyńskimi wydają z braku wygód i komfortu.

Walery Eljasz, 1874

Company which, while not very numerous is nevertheless more select than elsewhere, comes in the summer to Zakopane. People come here chiefly to tour the mountains or for intellectual recreation, while those who are abroad for business or amusement, who wish to put on airs, pretend to be great lords, or squander their estates go to the waters; for them the Tatras are a wilderness... Often encountering among the distinguished literary and artistic personalities in Zakopane a motley crowd of drawing-room dandies, I inquired into the reasons for their appearance on terrain so unpromising for them. My investigations convinced me that there was a fashion for it: one of the conditions of bon ton was at least once to pay a visit to the Tatras, which seemed so barbarian to them for want of comfortable conditions.

Walery Eljasz, 1874

Walery Eljasz
8. Zakopane z Gubałówki, (b.r.) 117 x 160 mm
8. *Zakopane from Gubałówka*, (n.d.) 117 x 160 mm

Przed nami, w górę, szedł skalny korytarz, między dwiema czarnymi ścianami granitu. W górze widniał biały płatek śniegu, ponad nim czerniła się skała i małe sylwetki podróżnych na tle jasnego nieba.
Stanisław Witkiewicz, 1891
In front of us, upwards, rose a corridor through the rocks, between two black granite faces. Above there glistened a white flake of snow, over it was the black rock with the small figures of the wanderers silhouetted against the bright sky *Stanisław Witkiewicz, 1891*

Walery lub (or) **Stanisław Eljasz**
106. Powrót od Morskiego Oka. Na koniu Walery Eljasz, obok góral Jakub Kluś z Olczy, 1891, 172 x 126 mm
106. Return to Lake Morskie Oko. Walery Eljasz mounted, with the Highlander Jakub Kluś of Olcza, 1891, 172 x 126 mm
Walery Eljasz
107. Wycieczka na Halę Gąsienicową, ok. 1894, 82 x 120 mm
107. Excursion to the mountain meadow Hala Gąsienicowa, c. 1894, 82 x 120 mm
108. Na Przełęczy Zawrat, 1893, 121 x 160 mm
108. On the Zawrat Pass, 1893, 121 x 160 mm
109. Rodzina Eljaszów z przewodnikami na Zawracie od strony Doliny Pięciu Stawów Polskich, 1893, 125 x 170 mm
109. The Eljasz family and guides on the Valley of the Five Polish Tarns side of the Zawrat, 1893, 125 x 170 mm
110. Córki Walerego Eljasza z Wacławem Anczycem i przewodnikami w Dolinie Pięciu Stawów Polskich, 1892, 110 x 155 mm
110. Walery Eljasz's daughters with Wacław Anczyc and guides in the Valley of the Five Polish Tarns, 1892, 110 x 155 mm

« Horowitz, Photographer ». 2003. Book and cover. Publisher: WAIF.

Tia i Rodya 1967

Dla artysty nie ma żadnego alibi

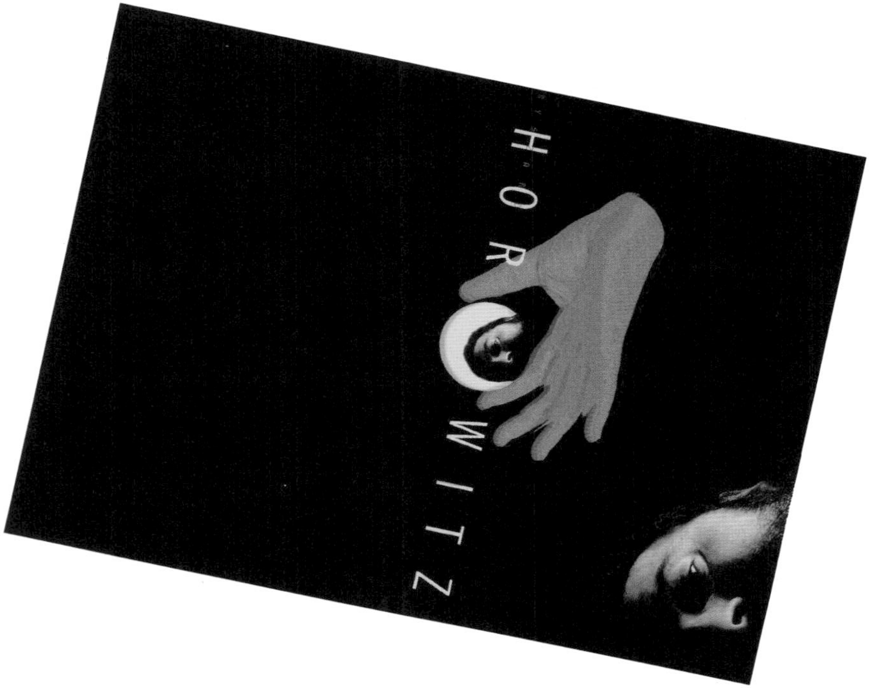

Od samego początku
jako narzędzie
Nie służące tylko i
do rejestrowania pejzaży
lecz również do kreowania
Moimi prekursorami są tak
duchów z końca dziewiętnastego
Oni nieźle oszukiwali. Posługując się
oświetleniem, wielokrotnym
rejestrowali dziwne efekty świetlne,
które potem sprzedawali jako zdjęcia
Każdy z nas
ma jakieś pragnienia,
marzenia,
gdy nie ma się
pragnień,
to się nie żyje.
Każdy więc chciałby,
jeżeli nie czegoś więcej,
to przynajmniej czegoś
innego.
Udało mi się
znaleźć zawód,
który łączy
przyjemne
W mojej pracy dość
wcześnie przestałem
interesować się fotografią
rejestrującą rzeczywistość.
Coraz bardziej pochłaniały
mnie działania wywodzące
się z malarskiej
rzeczywistości.
Nie fotografuję przedmiotu
jako takiego, tak
fotografuję własną
na ten temat.

pewnością

ne w mojej

wiadomości i stamtąd

przedostają się do prac.

Intryguje mnie świat, w którym wszystko staje się możliwe:

Apollonia 1985

fale morskie nieruchomieją, człowiek staje się ptakiem, koty fruwają, a piękne kobiety wyłaniają się ze ścian.

« Untitled ». Drawing.

« Theater ». 2004. Cover Calender. Client: Rzeszow Theatre.

« Praha ». 2003. Cover Calender. Publisher: J&S Group.

1 Śr / Wed
2 Czw / Thu
3 Pi / Fr
4 So / Sa
5 Ni / Su
6 Po / Mo
7 Wt / Tu
8 Śr / Wed
9 Czw / Thu
10 Pi / Fr
11 So / Sa
12 Ni / Su
13 Po / Mo
14 Wt / Tu
15 Śr / Wed
16 Czw / Thu
17 Pi / Fr
18 So / Sa
19 Ni / Su
20 Po/ Mo
21 Wt / Tu
22 Śr / Wed
23 Czw / Thu
24 Pi / Fr
25 So / Sa
26 Ni / Su
27 Po / Mo
28 Wt / Tu
29 Śr / Wed
30 Czw / Thu
31 Pi / Fr

Styczeń 2003 January

« Praha January ». 2003. Calender. Publisher: J&S Group.

« Wien march ». 2004. Calender. Publisher: J&S Group.

« Wien october ». 2004. Calender. Publisher: J&S Group.

The Warsaw Academy of Fine Arts

by Zdzislaw Schubert

The poster is unquestionably the most important discipline within all forms of graphic design. The attractiveness of this means of expression has always fascinated many artists and continues to do so, although it requires high intellectual standards and specialized knowledge. In the hundred years of the Warsaw Academy of Fine Arts the poster has played an important role in the curriculum and as an applied medium. This is especially true for the Department of Graphic Art, where poster design has been taught extensively and developed by outstanding artists who have worked there.

Partly as a result of coincidence and partly because of the way the teaching programmes have been jointly designed by the management and individual teachers, there have been periods when the department's work became known outside academia impacting artistic developments both in Poland and abroad.

At the beginning the way forward for graphic design in the academy was neither easy nor clear cut. In a hundred years the efforts to establish graphic design appropiately have met with variable fortune. Nevertheless, the teaching of graphic art both pure and applied has been recognized from the beginning of the academy's existence.

In 1922 separate Department of Graphics was established in the Warsaw Academy. It was headed by an outstanding graphic artist Wladyslaw Skoczylas. As well as teaching general subjects and various graphic techniques, the teaching programme also included lessons in applied graphics. Skoczylas wrote on the aims of the Academy: "We do not accept here that art can be divided into so called 'pure' art and so-called 'applied' art. We dream that our influence is seen in our lives, dominating the streets, penetrating temples and public buildings as well as a flat of a poor worker".

In 1923 another outstanding polish designer at the Department of Interior Design, Wojciech Jastrzebowski, was the first in the world to introduce studies in blocks and planes as a core subject to students of all years. This method of teaching was later followed in Sweden, Holland and Switzerland. The aim of providing an all-round education to students became an idiosyncratic feature which made the Warsaw Academy stand apart. These principles bore fruit particularly in the post war period and differentiated the Warsaw Academie art education system from the West, where there was a clear line between those schools where only fine art disciplines where taught, and those where designers were being educated for the needs of industry, advertising and media information.

In 1930 a separate Department of Applied Graphics was founded, which was headed by Edmund Bartlomiejczyk. The importance of this discipline increased substantially. Irrespective of their later specialization, students of graphic art had to study graphic design and vice versa. With such strong foundations many graduates practiced two or more disciplines simultaneously in their independent work.

On the whole this principle was continued, despite political system changes and the reorganization of the academy (which took place after the war). As a result of the 1952 reform of the Academy, two poster workshops were established. One was led by Henryk Tomaszewski, and the other by Józef Mroszczak. The works of these two professors had an enormous impact on the further development of the Department of Graphics.
Professor Tomaszewski said in the 60's. "In my workshop I would like to educated students to think logically, consistently and with the functionality of the design in mind. When I give them a subject, they should, by the way of analysis, discard what is redundant in order to get to the shortcut the sign. By the sign I understand the compression of form and subject. I try to make them give up statements, adjectives and all the beautiful but mostly redundant ornaments. I force them into asceticism and prefer the austerity than unnecessarily flowery work. I strive for the students to express their own opinions, be outspoken and independent in their vision, and stimulate their imagination. Be innovative". During work critiques Professor Tomaszewski was very emotionally involved and he often took the tools and placed corrections on the student's work. However, at the same time he did not enforce his way of thinking or his esthetics. The methods of Professor Tomaszewski emphasized the development of the intellectual sensitivity of the students rather than merely teaching them the sketching of the design.
From the point of view of their temperament and personality Professor Józef Mroszczak was nearly the exact opposite to Professor Tomaszewski. He was more restrained in his gestures, more balanced in his opinions and he evokes the peace and strength of his Highland pedigree. In a way, however, they both complemented each other. Mroszczak was above all the author of many pioneering efforts in Poland, seeking to increase the importance of graphic design in its wider context.
Mroszczak described in the following way the education methods in relation to Graphic Design: "The situation of Graphic Design, as far as the teaching method is concerned, is without precedence in Poland. We have given up narrow specialization in order to introduce the students to a broader understanding of all types of design. We lead them from analysis into the synthesis of all graphics disciplines, and we teach them versatility, flexibility and comprehensive thinking. Mroszczak also played an important role in setting up the International Biennale of the Poster in Warsaw, which he headed till his death in 1975.
The development of a strong graphics departments has been an ongoing process which continues to this day. Leszek Holdanowicz gave this process new impetus during his time as Dean of the Department from 1974 to 1980. Thanks to his efforts the department's current structure has been established to successfully meet the demands placed upon it by an ever-changing external environment. Building on the best of the academy's hundred-year-old tradition new teachers develop innovative solutions for this dynamically developing arena of visual communication. Today, on the top floor of the Graphic Department there are workshops for three teachers whose combined interests span across all the major areas of graphic design. Students have jokingly called them the BMW workshops - composed from the first letters of the professors' names - Maciej Buszewicz, Lech Majewski and Mieczyslaw Wasilewski.
Maciej Buszewicz leads the book workshop. In this field he has been awarded distinguished prizes in recognition of his innovative solutions in the area of shape and typography of books. Lech Majewski covers all aspects of publishing graphics. He is extremely competent and well-placed having had successes in this field. Furthermore he remains one of the most interesting poster designers of his generation with the ability to surprise the public every few years with fresh approaches to this visual language.
In turn Mieczyslaw Wasilewski continues to build on the work of his predecessors (Pofs. Tomaszewski and Palka) in the teaching of poster design, and he remains one of the most creative polish leaders of the discipline.

In order to demonstrate the methods used when working with students we will use the description of Maciej Buszewicz, which comes from his earlier work in the typography workshop of Prof. Lech Majewski: "The mission of the workshop is to teach graphic thinking with the use of typographic means only. One of the most significant and often determining moments in our work is the beginning phase, which is closer to literary analysis or an intellectual conversation on a literary subject than a critique in an art academy. Only after a comprehensive analysis of the piece is it possible to continue a disciplined graphic work.
In order to produce the required graphic-typographic form of the text students have to overcome many quality challenges. Irrespective of the students' intellectual qualities we have adopted a principle of randomly selecting the literary material to work on. It turns out that these tasks which present students with the most difficulties and which require them to overcome many barriers are the most satisfying for both parties. Most significantly it develops the student from within, which can easily be seen in their future work". As can be seen, the didactic work focuses on finding within each student their creative persona, so that they can deal with every situation they will face after graduating.
As mentioned earlier, Majewski develops, in his current workshop, a teaching methodology that focuses on the editorial form in its broad sense. Multimeditorial tasks can be categorized by students into a number of shapes, which can be integrated into the final editorial forms. The concept is then shaped by the author's own persona, and all the ideas have to be translated into a visual language. Among all those forms, the poster emerges only as one of the forms, not necessarily the dominating one. This approach to design is featured in other workshops too and it illustrates very well how far the teachers of the academy have come along this road over the last decades.
One can see that throughout all the changes, the main principle which inspired the founders of the academy from the beginning was carefully nurtured during the inter-war and post-war periods, and continues to be a central commitment for teachers today. We refer to the commitment to foster the spirit of the of humanities in such a way that students are given not only the specialized tools to do their job, but are also provided with a well-rounded education. During the whole educational process we pay attention to the students capabilities, in order to realize the potential which is dormant within each person and of which they themselves may not be aware.
More and more students graduate from the Department of Graphic Design and increasingly There is a geneational shift taking place amoung the teachers, and new demands of the job market. This process stretches over time but it is a stable trend. The complex face of the younger generation means quite a convoluted state of the art, where no single tendency is dominant.

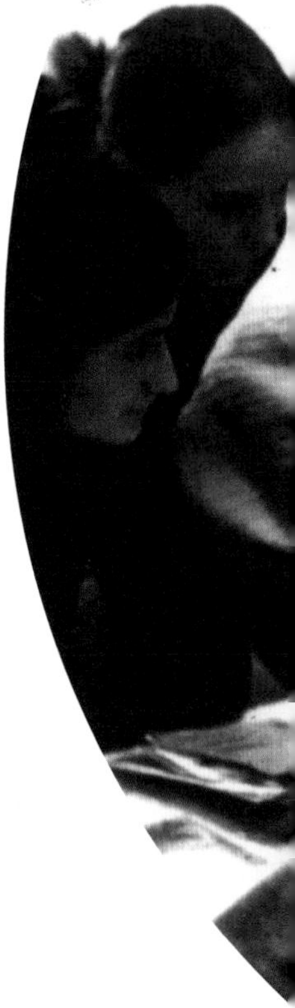

Zdżislaw Schubert
The curator of the Gallery of Poster and Design, National Museum in Poznan
"Welcome Warsaw" - Posters Exposition BMW /Buszewicz, Majewski, Wasilewski/
and their students from the Academy of Fine Arts Warsaw in Brussel, Belgium, 2005

ZA CHVILY TAM
JESTEM

DESIGNDESIGNER
IVENS FONTOURA

Termina em festa a Criação de Cartazes com Lech Majewski no MAA

Terminou em festa o curso **Criação de Cartazes** ministrado pelo designer gráfico polonês Lech Majewski, presente nas duas fotos (ao lado) junto com seus alunos.

São eles: Angela Maria Rosseto da Cruz, Adalberto Camargo, Adriana Salmazo, Alexis Morozowicz, Carla Beatriz Francho Ruschmann, Daniela Vicentini, Fernando Araya, Giorgia da Gama, Graziela Knabben, Julian Carlo Fagotti, Juliana Leonor Kudlinski, Juliana Dissenha, Leony de Souza Diotalevi, Livânia Pereira, Lucília Alencastro, Luiz Carlos Weiss, Marcia Selma Rodrigues, Maria Helena Fontana Cabral, Mari Ines Piekas, Rafael Piekarski Pereira, Richard Bischof, Rita Brandt Solieri, Rociane Furtado Araújo, Rosemeire Odahara, Sileny Ribeiro Arantes, Stely Marchesini, Suzana Mezzadri, Tania Machado, Vanessa Constance Ambrosio, Wesley Leal e Edwiges Maria Krzyzanowski.

Os alunos, a maioria graduados ou ainda estudantes do curso de Design Gráfico da Universidade Federal do Paraná, estão expondo o que produziram no MAA - Museu Alfredo Andersen, cuja mostra permanecerá aberta até 15 de março. A temática compõe-se de cinco itens, respectivamente, Carnaval, Gato, Happy New Year, Welcome e XV Oficina de Música de Curitiba.

Tanto o curso como a referida mostra fazem parte do projeto "Os brasileiros que vieram de

Nova APDesign no sul

Um grupo de designers gaúchos tomou a iniciativa e promoveu a reativação e o início pleno de atividades da APDI/RS, entidade que congrega os profissionais do design no Estado do Rio Grande do Sul, fundada em 1987. Depois de um intervalo inoperante, a entidade ressurge a partir do empenho de um grupo de profissionais, muitos dos quais pertencentes à antiga associação.

A nova razão social da entidade é resumida na expressão **APDesign, Associação dos Profissionais em Design do Rio Grande do Sul.**

A Associação tem como propósito a abrangente representação de seus sócios atuantes nos diferentes ramos como o design gráfico, de produto, de embalagem, de superfície, têxtil, calçados e acessórios, de interface, jóias, ambiental, de interiores, de ponto-de-venda, identidade corporativa, maquetes e protótipos, ergonomia, sinalização e áreas afins. Ela acolherá também sócios estudantes, honorários e colaboradores.

A diretoria eleita no dia 18 de novembro de 1995 para o período de um ano está assim constituída: presidente Sibelle Machado, vice-presidente Valpírio Monteiro, tesoureiro José Carlos Tonolli, secretária Letícia Albuquerque, diretoria de Capacitação Profissional Rubem Pechansky, diretoria de Ensino e Cultura Luiz Amaurety e diretoria de Relações Institucionais Marília Vianna.

Designdesigner cumprimenta pela significativa iniciativa e deseja profícua, gestão. Abaixo, reproduz na íntegra o documento **Carta de Porto Alegre,** de 19/8/95.

Carta de Porto Alegre

MISSÃO: "Afirmar o Design como uma forma autêntica de expressão social, econômica e cultural comprometida com a melhoria da qualidade de vida da sociedade como um todo".

OBJETIVOS PERMANENTES:

1 **Entidade Representativa:** Congregar profissionais em design no Estado do Rio Grande do Sul com o objetivo de representá-los como classe. 2. **Relação com o Mercado:** Incentivar as relações entre designers e indústria para que sejam gerados produtos mais criativos, com mais qualidade e com melhores condições de competir no Brasil e no exterior. 3. **Capacitação Profissional:** Estimular a qualificação técnico-cultural dos profissionais em design através da promoção de palestras, semi- estudo e programas de intercâmbio com entidades congêneres de outros estados. 4. **Vínculo com o Ensino:** Propiciar o estabelecimento de uma permanente relação entre as instituições de ensino do Design e a atividade profissional. 5. **Articulação e Fomento:** Atuar junto as instituições financiadoras de desenvolvimento tecnológico e científico no sentido de adoção de programas de pesquisa e desenvolvimento do Design. 6. **Melhoria da Qualidade de Vida:** Discutir com a comunidade iniciativas que representem melhoria da qualidade de vida da sociedade como um todo. 7. **Divulgação do Design:** Funcionar como entidade informadora, mediadora e crítica junto à sociedade com relação a assuntos referentes a design. 8. **Direito Auto-**

JOGO RÁPIDO

• **O arcanjo**

De dançarino de "Embalos de sábado à noite" e assassino frio de "Pulp fiction" a arcanjo Miguel. O ator John Travolta foi tentado a aceitar o papel no filme "Miguel" por Nora Ephron, pois não será uma figura etérea, pura e santa, como poderiam esperar os mais desavisados. O arcanjo Miguel é um bêbado mulherengo, que vive em Iowa com sua mulher (Andie McDowell). Em seu encalço está um jornalista que de tanto forçar acaba conseguindo desvendar toda a história e leva um susto com o par de asas de Travolta.

• **Pandora**

Neste sábado, a banda curitibana Pandora faz sua estréia no palco do AeroAnta, de Ponta Grossa. Com Flávio no vocal, Thomas na guitarra, Luciano no baixo, Arnoldo na bateria e Alvaro no teclado, a Banda Pandora, conta com três anos de estrada e se caracteriza pelos seus diversos estilos, e traz em seu repertório o melhor do pop, reggae e rock. (Ingressos a seis reais com direito a uma cerveja).

• **Teatro**

O domínio dos computadores limita criação de cartazes

Joseane Martins

Os computadores, pela lógica, chegaram para facilitar a vida das pessoas. No entanto, usado inadequadamente eles podem levar a limitação da criatividade. Pelo menos é o que garante o artista polonês Lech Majewski, que está ministrando no Museu Alfredo Andersen o curso de criação de cartazes. "As agências estão unificando o trabalho computador/artista. E não é assim. O computador deve ser só um instrumento de ajuda, ele não pode e não deve substituir o artista", critica.

Essa limitação de criatividade tem sido uma das maiores dificuldades dos artistas brasileiros. "Temos no Brasil bons cartazes, mas os brasileiros não aprenderam ainda a dar importância à expressão do artista, muitas vezes nem ele sabe de seu potencial", constata. Por isso, o curso tem por objetivo aperfeiçoar o lado criativo dos alunos. "É preciso despertar dentro do artista a liberdade de criação, e é isso que eu tento tirar dos meus alunos", diz.

Para Lech Majewski, a ten-

Segundo o professor, há dois tipos de cartaz: "A arte de rua, que tem por objetivo informar, animar e incentivar; e o cartaz artístico, que vai aos museus e galerias". O primeiro tipo geralmente é encomendado, o que limita a criatividade de quem o faz. "Quem encomenda acaba fazendo restrições. Não que não fique um trabalho bonito, mas está longe do que o artista realmente gostaria de fazer sobre o assunto".

Este outro tipo de limitação vem sendo sentido por Lech Majewski nos designers brasileiros. "Muitos deles têm vontade e podem se tornar artistas, mas é preciso que eles se soltem mais, deixem o interior falar mais alto". Já o segundo tipo, o artístico, é o que tem grande importância na Polônia. "Lá as pessoas procuram interpretar as expressões e sentimentos mais puros do artista, que acaba ficando mais consciente disso", diferencia. Os próprios alunos do curso, quando descobrem o potencial artístico, chegam a se surpreender. "Eles são habilidosos, mas muitas vezes

Lech Majewski e os cartazes poloneses: criatividade.

países, foram selecionados para integrar o evento.

Os cartazes elaborados pelos 33 alunos durante o período do curso ficarão expostos no Museu Alfredo Andersen de 16 de feve-

Festa de polaco

Lech Majewski — cartazista polonês — expõe na cidade e dá curso para artistas plásticos no Alfredo Andersen.

José Carlos Fernandes

O sobrenome não causaria estranheza em nenhuma lista telefônica de Curitiba: Majewski. O nome remete a alguém famoso: Lech. Seria Lech Walesa? A imagem sugere, mas não é. O artista polonês Lech Majewski chegou há pouco à polaca capital paranaense para ministrar um curso aos artistas locais. Expoente das artes plásticas em seu país e divulgador do cartaz há muitas primaveras, ele vem se entrosando com a gente daqui para melhor desenvolver seu trabalho. Prazer em conhecê-los! "É preciso descobrir as próprias raízes", insiste, sem medo da palavra tradição, da qual tira o ranço e trata como passagem obrigatória rumo à auto-expressão. Bem-humorado e informal, Lech deu uma entrevista exclusiva ao **Caderno G.**

O senhor é um dos organizadores da Bienal Internacional de Cartaz. Como pode ser avaliado este evento?

É a bienal de cartaz mais importante do mundo, em funcionamento há 30 anos. Muitos dos artistas mais influentes da atualidade — no ramo do cartaz — um dia mostraram seus trabalhos ali. Ganhar um prêmio em Varsóvia é a maior honra no meio gráfico. A seleção é bastante rigorosa, pois chegam a ser mandados dois mil cartazes de mais ou menos sessenta países. São aceitos 400 trabalhos, em média. Em 1996 a abertura vai acontecer no dia 8 de junho. Além da exposição principal, acontecem mais ou menos 50 eventos paralelos, entre mostras de cinema, pintura, workshops, seminários... Lembro-me de alguns brasileiros que dela participaram, como Felipe Taborda.

Algum elemento histórico ou social, na sua opinião, determina sobremaneira a convergência dos artistas poloneses às artes gráficas?

É uma questão de mentalidade. A alma polaca é muito romântica. Além do mais, no meu país os artistas se ocupam de produzir cartazes. Importa muito interpretação sobre um determinado tema, e não apenas a comunicação de uma mensagem, de forma seca, dura, suscinta. O cartaz polonês tradicionalmente se nutre de alusões, comentários e às vezes se serve da provocação. Cada cartazista cria seu próprio estilo. Por essas e outras, a produção polonesa acabou sendo diferente de todas as outras. Seu desenvolvimento maior deu-se nos anos 50/60 e logo surgiu o título de "escola polonesa de cartaz", uma vez que passou a influenciar criadores de inúmeros países. Gente de todas as partes foi à Polônia aprender nossas técnicas.

Qual a relação que o regime comunista tinha com os artistas poloneses? De alguma maneira o cartaz — entendido como um gênero popular — foi incentivado pelo poder naquele momento?

Todo mundo fica chocado ao saber que no tempo do comunismo era possível fazer uma arte tão livre. Na Polônia o regime não se metia na arte. Situações muito piores enfrentaram os colegas dos países capitalistas, uma vez que as campanhas publicitárias e as pessoas do mundo dos negócios, nesses lugares, encomendavam cartazes e tentavam manipular a criação. Não tínhamos problema algum nesse sentido. O comunismo polonês era muito diferente do soviético. Por causa disso foi possível acabar com ele.

Qual o grau de atenção que o regime tinha para com os artistas? Alguns ateliês eram financiados? E hoje...

Não existia na Polônia um comunismo como o que se lê nos livros. Mas havia censura aos artistas, é verdade. Por causa dessa condição, os cartazistas acabaram se servindo de metáforas, alusões diversas e empregaram linguagens mais subjetiva. As mensagens acabavam ficando sempre nas entrelinhas.

No Brasil há uma estranha distinção entre o artista e o ilustrador, em detrimento do segundo. Situação semelhante ocorre em seu país no que se refere aos cartazistas? Faz sentido falar em "arte menor"?

Acho que essas divisões do século 20 são muito esquisitas. Elas decorrem de pessoas que não entendem o significado da arte. Se nós temos um pintor muito fraco e um ilustrador muito bom, qual deles seria o artista? Se estivéssemos no século 25, na certa iríamos olhar não para o pintor ruim, mas para o bom ilustrador. Podemos encontrar cartazes em museus de arte moderna de Nova York, lugares em que apenas são aceitas obras de arte verdadeiramente. Ali não de faz distinção entre a pintura em tela e o resto.

O gênero cartaz se aproxima bastante da publicidade, comumente desprezada pelos que se dedicam às artes no seu sentido clássico... E para Lech, existe este conflito?

Na verdade, todo o cartaz é publicitário, pois se destina a ilustrar de exposições e peças de teatro a propagandas de água mineral... Lidar com tudo isso vai depender da coragem daquele que faz o trabalho e da ousadia de quem encomenda. Comumente os cartazes de publicidade são muito parecidos. Atribuo isto à mentalidade dos empresários. É muito mais fácil para eles colocar uma fotografia e escrever algo sobre ela.

O que determina o cartaz enquanto linguagem? Existe algo que o distingue de outras formas de expressão?

É difícil responder isso porque tudo pode ser um cartaz. Qualquer um deles revela sempre uma informação. Uma pintura não foge disso. A diferença, em ambos os casos, é que um artista está passando esse recado. Digo mais: mesmo um quadro de Rembrandt, Matisse, Van Gogh e outros podem ser convertidos em cartaz.

Fale sobre seu processo criativo. Qual sua matéria-prima fundamental?

De tempos em tempos modifico as técnicas. Na arte, cada ser humano muda a cada cinco anos, mais ou menos. Procuro pensar na concepção do trabalho, mas me sirvo de instrumentos livres e diferentes. Transito pela gravura e lanço mão da fotografia. Ultimamente andei misturando um pouco de tudo isso e meu trabalho passou a figurar entre os cem cartazes mais importantes do mundo, segundo uma publicação japonesa. Destes, inclusive, onze são poloneses.

O cartazista, pela destinação do que produz, deve se preocupar mais com o espectador, evitando formas de expressão muito herméticas ou sofisticadas?

Como podemos aceitar o que não entendemos? Se eu falo em polonês e o interlocutor não conhece nada dessa língua, isso faz algum sentido? Na arte é a mesma coisa. O artista fala para que as pessoas o compreendam. Se eu não identifico do que se trata uma imagem, não a aceito. Isso não significa que qualquer pessoa entenda o cartaz. Ele, como outras obras de arte, não é dirigido a todos. Mozart vai interessar aos que gostam dele e não àqueles que escutam com fone de ouvidos enquanto comem pipocas... (risos)

O senhor poderia apresentar as linhas-mestras do curso que ministra a 30 artistas de Curitiba?

Os participantes receberam temas individuais e por intermédio dessa atividade estamos tentando encontrar a personalidade de cada um. Estamos lutando contra a unificação e as estruturas impostas, coisas que são ruins para a arte. Quero achar nessas pessoas as características mais importantes que elas carregam consigo. Não é o mais importante se nós estamos ou não fazendo cartaz. Estamos apenas no começo do trabalho e já dá para ver que muitas idéias interessantes estão aparecendo. O importante é se desvencilhar do que foi colocado na cabeça de cada um como se fosse uma regra.

O senhor já recolheu alguma impressão sobre a arte do cartaz no Brasil?

O cartaz brasileiro se utiliza muito pouco daquilo que é a tradição do país. De um certa maneira é superficial demais e ele são parecidos em demasia uns com os outros. Nem sempre dá para ver que um artista o produziu. **(colaboração de Dulce Osinski, Jadzia e Palulis)**

Serviço: Cartazes Poloneses. Exposição com exemplares de vários artistas da Polônia. Museu Alfredo Andersen (Rua Mateus Leme, 336). Permanece até 15 de fevereiro.

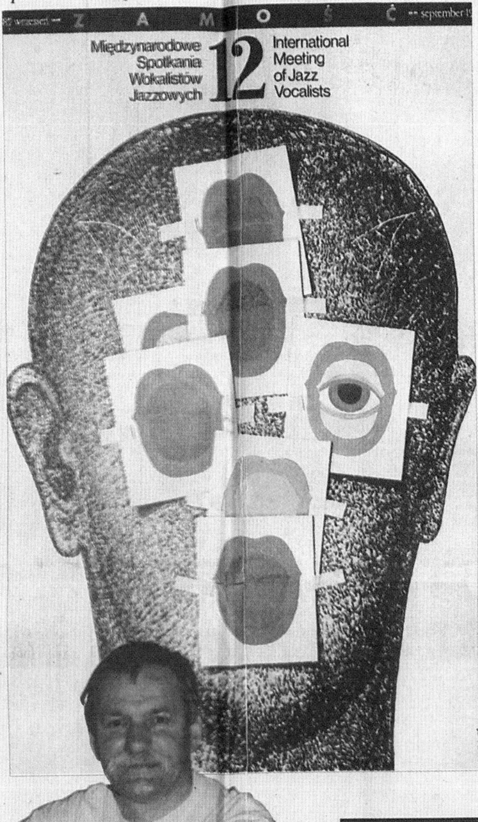

"A alma polaca é muito romântica. No meu país os artistas se ocupam de produzir cartazes. Nossa arte tradicionalmente se nutre de alusões, comentários e às vezes se serve da provocação". Lech Wajewski

Ele tem o maior cartaz

Lech Majewski é daquelas figuras simples, que senta ao chão para ser entrevistado. Sincero, devolve sem cerimônias algumas perguntas e transforma tudo num bate-papo. Por conta de sua informalidade, nada denuncia a importância que ele ocupa no cenário das artes plásticas polonesas. E por que não dizer mundiais. Em Nova York, Paris ou Amsterdã, não importa, os museus renomados do planeta possuem um cartaz de Majewski. A identificação desse artista que pinta, grava, serigrafa, desenha... com o cartaz pode causar estranheza aos brasileiros, pouco afeiçoados a esse gênero. Daí a importância da exposição "Cartazes Poloneses", da qual Lech faz parte. Ela nos educa.

Publicidades de produtos industriais, culturais e o que mais pintar no pedaço — todos tratados com o requinte de linguagens artísticas — só pode ser mesmo coisa boa de ver. Não que a propaganda brasileira seja desprezível ou deficiente. Pelo contrário. Mas ainda, em terras tupiniquins, não se vê comumente gente renomada do mundo da arte embrenhada no "famigerado" universo da compra e venda. Majewski não se detém nestas questões e passa mesmo a impressão que elas não lhe pertencem. Por essas e outras, a conversa avança e a interação se torna ainda mais rica e eficaz. E ainda mais: o artista nos fala com a mesma intensidade dos seus feitos sobre encomenda e do que criou no momento de mais profunda interioridade. Um momento e outro ele resume numa palavra: ousadia. Palavras ao vento. Seus cartazes, por si só, dão testemunho dessa postura.

Lech Jerzy Majewski nasceu em 1947 na cidade de Olstyn, Polônia. Cursou academia de Belas Artes em Varsóvia. Além da dedicação às artes plásticas, faz as vezes de pesquisador no campo do cartaz, assunto do qual diz "saber tudo", com a propriedade de quem acompanha uma bienal internacional exclusiva para esse gênero. Sua obra gráfica concentra-se principalmente na ilustração de livros didáticos, embora não sejam poucas suas incursões pelo design cinematográfico e a própria publicidade. **(JCF)**

1.) Besancon exhibition. 2001.
2.) Ryszard Kajzer ex-assistent.
3.) Majewski with Mietek Wasilewski and students from Brasil.
4.) Wasilewski, Myjak, Buszewicz and Majewski in Rio de Janeiro.
5.) Exhibition in Galerie Grenette. Sion. Switzerland. 1994.
6.) Hotel de Ville in Besancon. Lech Majewski with Alain Philpe.
7.) Wasilewski and Majewski in Rio de Janeiro.
8.) Exposition in Maison d'Image. Brussel.
9.) BMW (Buszewicz, Majewski, Wasilewski).

1

2

3

4

9

5

6

7

8

1

2

3

4

5

6

1.) Exposition in Maison d'image.
2.) Thierry Sarfis and Majewski in Maison d'Image in Brussel.
3.) Lech Majewski, Krzysztof Ducki. Sandor Pinczehelyi. Hungary 2006. Exhibition.
4.) Ola Kot, Justyna Czerniakowska, Lech Majewski.
5.) Magda Ciesielska, Lech Majewski, Magda Kurpik. Poster Biennale in Warsaw.
6.) Eugeniusz Lukasiak. Graphik Design Assistent in Studio.

7.) Assistents: Justyna Czerniakowska, Ewa Engler, Ola Kot, Ryszard Kayzer.
8.) Justyna Czerneiakowska, Lech Majewski, Ola Kot.
9.) Opening Exhibition Hungaria. 2006.
10.) Lech Majewski in Cambodja.
11.) Lech Majewski with Helmut Bauer and Paulina Gancarczyk in Munich. (Paulina is a graphic designer, assistent in studio).
12.) Graphic designer Edyta Majewska. Daughter of Lech Majewski.

7

8

9

10

11

12

1.) Uwe Loesch and Lech Majewski.
2.) Lech Majewski. Opening ceremony. Poster Biennale in Warsaw. 2006.
3.) Buszewicz, Loesch, Wasilewski. Poster Biennale in Warsaw. 2006.
4.) Meeting at Michel Batory. 2005.
5.) Kot, Czerniakowska and Majewski in Kafka Museum in Prague.
6.) Diplom Natalia Gosciniak.

7.) Lech Majewski, Pagowska Tomasilewski and Wasilewski.
8.) Lech Majewski and Finn Nygaard. Poster Biennale in Warsaw. 2006.
9.) Diplom Justyna Czerniakowska.
10.) Diplom Agnieszka Kucharska. 2005.
11.) Diplom Ola Kot. 2005.
12.) Diplomants. 2005.

1

2

3

4

5

6

7

8

9

10

11

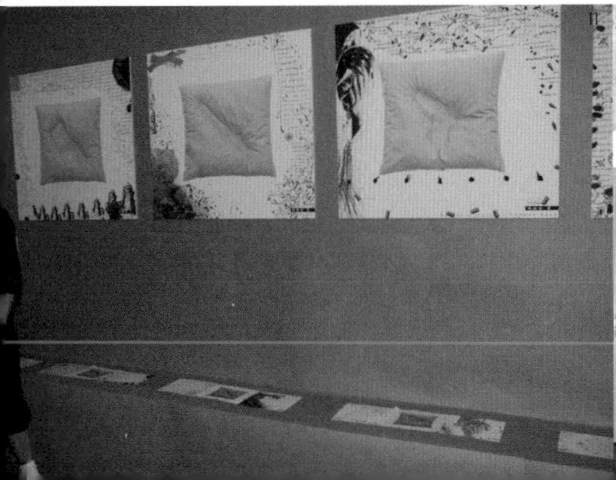

12

Lech Majewski

Born in 1947, in Olsztyn.

Graduated from the Faculty of Graphics at Academy of Fine Arts in Warsaw. Diploma in 1972 at the studio of Professor Henryk Tomaszewski. At present, he is a professor in the same academy and also acts as the President of the Organizing Committee of the International Poster Biennale in Warsaw. Works as a graphic artist in the area of poster and book design, as well as book ilustrations. He has held lectures and workshops in many universities throughout the world.

Awards

1971 second prize in International Poster Competition to Celebrate 25th anniversary of Unesco.

1980 distinction in "The Hollywood Reporter's" competition for the world best film poster in Los Angeles.

1981 1st Prize at UN competition.

1983 Grand Prix, the Silver Medal and the Special Prize at the Xth BPP in Katowice.

1984 Special Prize at IX/Xth International Poster Biennale in Warsaw.

1985 1st Prize in a poster contest "Sobriety-Culture-Security".

1st Prize in a poster competition on "Fire-Fighting".

1986 Polish Prime Minister's award, along with K. Syta for creative achievements for the youth, namely, book design of maths textbook for 1st graders.

1987 1st Prize in "International Chopin Contest" poster competition.

IInd award of IInd International Poster Salon in Paris for "XIIIth Meetings of Jazz Vocalist" poster.

Special Prize of XIIth Biennale of Polish Poster in Katowice for the "Beware of Viper" film poster.

1st Prize in the 1986 Warsaw Best Poster Warsaw contest for film poster "A Story of Gloomy Mountain".

Polish Book Publishers' award for "Best Book Design" of 1986.

1989 award of Polish Book Publishers for "Best Book Design" of 1988 for a Polish textbook for 1st graders "Letters".

1st Prize, along with Maciej Buszewicz, in International "Best Record Cover Design" competition of the 1989 Sopot Song Contest for "Komeda" album.

1990 IIIrd award of the Przemysl All-Poland survey of "Museum and Relics' Protection Poster" for "Bicentenary of French Revolution".

Award of Czech Minister of Culture at XIVth Biennale of Graphic Design in Brno for a set of posters.

2000 1st Prize in Poster festival in Krakow, Poland.

2003 Prize of the ICOGRADA in Poster Triennale in Trnava, Slovakia.

2003 1st Prize in the Calendar Competition for calendar "Prague 2003".

2004 1st Prize in the Calendar Competition for calendar "Wien 2004".

1996 - 2004 Awards of Polish Book Publishers for "Best Book Design".

Lectures and workshops:

The Minerva Academy of Fine Arts, Groningen, Holland; Academy of Fine Arts, Arnhem, Holland; The Rovaniemi Institut of Arts and Handicrafts, Rovaniemi, Finland; Instituto Europeo di Design, Torino, Italy; Faculdad de Artes Plasticas Universidad Veracruzana, Xalapa, Mexico; L'Ecole Profesional Art Contemporain, Sion, Switzerland; HDK, Berlin, Germany; Center of Modern Art, Curitiba, Brasil; International Poster Art, Torino, Italy; Ecole Regionale Beaux Artes, Besançon, France; University's in Chile: La Serena, Vina del Mar, Santagio; Internationale Poster Biennale, San Luis Potosi, Mexico; University of Arts, Saigon, Vietnam; REYUM, Phnom Penh, Kambodia; Ecal Intuit/Lab, Paris, France; "Mois du Graphisme", Echirolles, France.

One-man shows

1981 Dom Artysty Plastyka in Warsaw, Poland

1984 Pécs Gallery in Hungary

1987 Clermont Ferrand, France

1989 Polish Culture Center in Prague, Czechoslovakia

1990 Gröningen, Holland

1991 Täysikuu, Finland

1992 Zamosc, Poland

1992 Hrubieszów, Poland

1994 Rio de Janeiro, Brasil

1994 Halapa, Mexico

1995 La Grenette in Sion, Switzerland
1996 Curitiba, Brasil
1997 Usti nad Labem, Czech
1999 Rzeszow, Poland
2000 "Mois du Graphisme", Echirolles, France
2001 "Plakrak" in Krakow, Poland
2001 Galerie Hutel de V.ille, Besançone, France
2001 Galeria Universidad La Serena, Chile
2001 Museo Bellas Artes, Vina del Mar, Chile
2001 Galeria Universidad Diego Posrtales, Santiago, Chile
2002 Gallery Bemowo, Warsaw, Poland
2003 Halapa, Mexico
2003 "Praha 2003", Dom Holenderski, Gdansk, Poland
2003 "Praha 2003", Praha, Czech
2004 "Wien 2004", Warsaw, Poland
2004 Rzeszow, Poland
2004 Saigon, Vietnam
2004 Phnom Penh, Kambodia
2004 Rzeszow, Poland
2004 Galeria Plakatu i Grafiki, Warsaw, Poland
2004 "Mois du Grahpisme", Grenoble, France
2005 "Bmw", Brussels, Belgium

Exhibitions

The Polish Poster Biennale in Katowice
The International Poster Biennale in Warsaw
The International Poster Triennial in Toyama
The Poster Biennale in Colorado, USA
The Poster Biennale in Lahti, Finland
The International Poster Biennale in Helsinki
The International Poster Salon in Paris
The International Biennale of Design in Brno
The Poster Festival in Pecs, Hungary
The Theatre Poster Biennale in Osnabruck, Germany
The poster exhibition in Rio de Janeiro, Brasil
The poster exhibition in Grugldiasco, Italy
"Warsaw's Best Poster" – annual exhibitions
The Poster Festival in Chaumont, France
The Graphic Month in Echirolle, France
The poster Biennale in Mexico
"The most beautiful book of the year"
The International Competition for the best record cover

Vision of Design: Lech Majewski

Edited and Distributed in Europe and Latin America by:
Index Book S.L.
Consell de Cent 160, local 3
08015 Barcelona
Tel: +34 93 454 5547
Fax: +34 93 454 8438
Email: ib@indexbook.com
www.indexbook.com

Editor: Jianping He
Concept & Selection of images:
Lech Majewski, Jianping He
Design & layout: Jianping He
Staff: Annika Wolfzettel
Contact & arrangement:
Sonny Kim-He
Paulina Gancarczyk
Proofreading:
Bettina Andrianantoandro,
Peter Walton

Cover and imprint design for Europe and Latin America edition:
EMEYELE (www.emeyele.com)

ISBN 978-84-96774-01-8

Printed and bound by:
SNP Leefung Printers
(Shenzhen) Co., Ltd.